Preface

The one hundredth anniversary of The Commercial Appeal, which this booklet commemorates, finds two of America's most famous journalistic institutions united, for The Commercial Appeal today is one of the family of Scripps-Howard Newspapers. The ideals and the spirit that motivated the one are found to be an integral part of the other. Each grew from small beginnings.

In November, 1878, the late E. W. Scripps founded in Cleveland, Ohio, a small newspaper that he called "The Penny Press," which marked both a new era and a new concept in American journalism. He dedicated his paper to the plain people and became the champion of these hitherto voiceless millions in their cause for social justice, greater opportunities and improvement of the American standard of living.

On that sure foundation grew The Cleveland Press—as it is now called—and its sister newspapers that E. W. Scripps soon started in other cities. Today, the Scripps-Howard Newspapers span the United States from New York to San Francisco, and prominent among them is The Commercial Appeal which became a member of the Scripps-Howard family when it was purchased by that organization in September, 1936.

Thus it is that today we find two of America's most venerable journalistic institutions united—a newspaper that has served the MidSouth faithfully for one hundred years, and an organization whose progressive policies are now accepted practice.

This was our first office, our first editor—and here is how Editor Henry Van Pelt (inset) chronicled the news of Andrew Jackson's death in his Memphis Weekly Appeal on June 14, 1845.

ONE HUNDRED YEARS

of

THE COMMERCIAL APPEAL

By ROBERT TALLEY
Editor, The Centennial Edition

*The Story Of The Greatest Romance
In American Journalism
1840 To 1940*

Printed At The Commercial Appeal
Copyright, 1940, by The Memphis Publishing Co.

Introduction

The Commercial Appeal issues this souvenir booklet on the occasion of its one hundredth anniversary, which was featured by the publication of its 328-page Centennial Edition on Jan. 1, 1940.

An institution which endures for a century must have qualities that are deep rooted in the life of its community. It must have served a need and served that need faithfully. We are proud that we can commemorate, in this booklet, such a long span of public service.

But it is not merely our own achievements, however, upon which we intend to dwell in these pages, for the Story of The Commercial Appeal is but a part of a far greater story, The Story of Memphis and the MidSouth.

The real history of any newspaper is the history of the community which it serves, for the fortunes of the two are inseparable. For a hundred years—through Civil War and yellow fever, through peace and plenty and through panic and prosperity—The Commercial Appeal has been the faithful friend and loyal servant of five generations of MidSouth readers, newspaper and reader sharing their fortunes in good times and bad.

Thus we present herewith The Story of Memphis and the MidSouth for the past one hundred years, through which runs The Story of The Commercial Appeal like a silken thread in a garment that is a century old.

THE COMMERCIAL APPEAL.
"The South's Greatest Newspaper"

Memphis, 1940.

The Contents

Chapter		Page
I	A NEWSPAPER IS BORN	1
II	"BEFO' DE WAH"	8
III	"THE GREATEST REBEL OF THEM ALL"	16
IV	A HOMELESS WANDERER	25
V	ATLANTA—AND SHERMAN	31
VI	JOURNEY'S END	37
VII	THE ROAD BACK	44
VIII	YELLOW FEVER DAYS	50
IX	THE MOONEY ERA	59
X	DOWN TO NOW	66

Appendix

"God Bless Memphis," Wept Mark Twain	I
"The Birth of a New Nation"	III
The Appeal Battery In Civil War	V
The Appeal's Yellow Fever Dead	VI
"Jesus, The Perfect Man"	VII

ACKNOWLEDGMENT

To the many persons who have co-operated by providing material for this booklet, and especially to Albert Johnson, head of the Reference Department of Cossitt Library, who labored most assiduously with me amid the old files, the author herewith makes grateful acknowledgment.

—Printed in the U. S. A.

Herein begins the Story of The Commercial Appeal, in the world of a hundred years ago. It has left its mark upon that world ever since.

CHAPTER I

A Newspaper Is Born

IT WAS a long, long time ago—a hundred years, to be exact. Martin Van Buren was president of the United States, the dazzling light that had been Andrew Jackson was now a feeble flame as it burned to its end amid the quiet shades of the Hermitage. England's girl-queen, Victoria, was just beginning her long reign that was destined to last 63 years. Still alive were men who had shaken hands with George Washington.

Today's world was in the making.

The Battle of New Orleans was a memory of only 25 years past. The Mexican War was still six years ahead, the War Between the States a full generation in the future. Only recently had the Indians, under guard of Federal soldiers, been removed from their tribal lands in the MidSouth to what was then Indian Territory and what is now Oklahoma.

Life was as primitive as the times—and as hard.

Memphis was a lusty little river hamlet of not quite 1800 souls that clung precariously to the tall Chickasaw Bluffs near the mouth of Wolf River, an island of safety when the Spring floods rolled down the broad Mississippi and spread their tawny blankets over the surrounding lowlands for hundreds of square miles. On its narrow streets that ran between the rows of low wooden houses—boot-deep in mud after every heavy rain—pioneers in buckskin shirts and coonskin caps, fresh from bear hunts and turkey shoots, still were to be seen. The more elegant gentlemen wore long frock coats, chin whiskers and bucket-sized beaver hats as they twirled their gold-headed canes; the ladies were dreams of dainty loveliness in their saucy bonnets ornamented with roses and pink ribands, their balloon sleeves and their voluminous dresses that bore the shape of a dinner bell and often concealed four silken petticoats and a pair of lace-trimmed pantalets as well.

On the east, the cotton fields came up to meet the city limits at Bayou Gayoso and beyond lay the great plantations. Among the largest was that of Geraldus Buntyn, crusty but pious Baptist, whose big manor house stood near the present site of the Memphis Country Club and who preached each Sunday morning to his hundred black slaves. Others included the old Holmes plantation whose great mansion with its tall Tuscan columns and quaint dormer windows frowned sternly over the present Chulahoma Road; also, the Enoch Ensley Plantation on Horn Lake Road, now owned by Dover Barrett.

These plantations were practically self-sufficient units. The forest and the saw mill turned out the lumber for the buildings; the grist mill, turned by water, ground the corn into meal for bread; the cattle furnished the meat, leather, milk and butter; the vineyards supplied the wine for candle-lit tables; the sheep yielded the wool and the cotton the cloth. Within the great mansion lived the planter and his family, fringing it were the slave quarters with their white-washed cabins and tiny garden plots.

It was a distant day—a day that is now but a dim memory.

Years were to elapse before the coming of the railroad and the first brassy neigh of the "Iron Horse" was to echo in the Mississippi Valley. Samuel Morse's "electric telegraph," patented only that year, was still an inventor's filmy dream. Such things as the electric light, the telephone, the automobile, the airplane and the radio were undreamed of mysteries of the future in the unknown world that lay ahead.

Into that strange world of 100 years ago—the world of 1840 —The Commercial Appeal was born.

Day by day, every day, this newspaper has mirrored the progress of a century. It has been the morning news diet of five generations of readers in the MidSouth, as welcome—and as necessary—at their breakfast tables as their cup of steaming coffee.

A Newspaper Is Born

The story of a great section and a great newspaper have been as one. Since the days when antebellum life flowered with its wealth and its ease and its chivalry, through the grim years of the Civil War, through the tragic era of reconstruction and carpetbag rule when the devastated South struggled to rise from its ashes, through the ghastly yellow fever epidemic of 1878 that almost depopulated Memphis, through the World War and down to now, The Commercial Appeal and the MidSouth have shared their common fortunes in good times as well as bad. Today, as it did a hundred years ago, this newspaper daily holds aloft its mirror to reflect the life of the region that it serves and captures the image on the printed page for the benefit of both present and posterity.

The Commercial Appeal is the lineal descendant of the first Democratic newspaper published in Memphis and its long and honorable career stretches back almost to the birth of the city itself. Its ancestral line retreats to a four-page, four-column weekly that was published in the pioneer hamlet of Memphis and which was known as "The Western World and Memphis Banner of the Constitution"—but let's begin at the beginning.

It is late in the year 1840. The great financial panic of 1837 has tossed the aged Gen. William Henry Harrison, who had been somewhat of a hero of the War of 1812, into the presidential chair. He is a Whig and his victory is a bitter morsel for the Democratic orators and newspapers who have assailed him as a dotard and a granny, one who should be content with a log cabin and a barrel of hard cider instead of aspiring to the White House. Out of this has come the historic "Log Cabin and Hard Cider Campaign" and President Martin Van Buren, Gen. Andrew Jackson's protege and idol of the Southern Democrats, has been defeated for re-election.

The news of General Harrison's victory has just been received by steamboat and in a little wooden building near the muddy banks of Wolf River an editor sits amid his dusty type cases and Washington hand press as he bends over his desk. He scribbles with a quill pen by the light of a tallow candle for he is writing an editorial, an editorial that is destined to leave its mark upon the city and his community for a century to come.

It is unfortunate that no copy of this editorial is now extant, but knowing its nature and its purpose we can easily surmise and paraphrase what it said. It read something like this:

"Martin Van Buren, that estimable Democrat and eminent statesman, has been defeated for re-election to the presidency by Gen. William Henry Harrison, a Whig. As editor of The Western World and Memphis Banner of the Constitution, we have, as our readers well know, loyally supported Mr. Van Buren throughout his campaign for re-election.

"The Whigs have been victorious but the Democrats have not been vanquished, as time will prove. We agree with Mr. Van Buren's statement that 'The sober second thought of the people is never wrong, and always efficient.' It is with this fact in mind—that the sober second thought of the people is never wrong—that this newspaper now appeals to the people to reverse their decision in the recent election and, in the next election, return a Democrat to the presidential chair.

"To encourage and abet this sober second thought of the people, and to appeal for a reversal, we are hereby changing the name of this newspaper to The Memphis Appeal, and by this name it henceforth will be known."

And so, The Memphis Appeal was born a hundred years ago. For a century it has been the MidSouth's mighty river of journalism into which a score or more tributary journals have flowed until today—after numerous mergers, purchases and consolidations—it still lives as The Commercial Appeal.

The editor who made that historic decision back in 1840, and thus became the founder of The Memphis Appeal, was Col. Henry Van Pelt, whom Keating and other historians have called "the father of Memphis journalism." He was the first of a long line of notable editors who have served this newspaper and the MidSouth for a hundred years.

We get a picture of Colonel Van Pelt's pioneer era when, turning the brittle pages of the yellowed old files, we read in The Appeal of Feb. 14, 1845, that he was offering subscriptions to the paper in return for vegetables, chickens and milk.

His announcement said:

"Having recently commenced housekeeping, we would say to those residing in the vicinity who may wish to take The Appeal and prefer paying in the produce of their farms, gardens, dairies, etc., that all articles consumed in the family will be taken in payment for subscriptions."

Likewise we read that in appreciation of Editor Van Pelt's vigorous support of James K. Polk in the presidential campaign of 1844 an enthusiastic West Tennessee admirer presented him with a hand-made hickory chair. Appropriate enough, it seems, in view of the editor's continued staunch advocacy of "Old Hickory's" vigorous Democratic principles.

Editor Van Pelt's Memphis was the Memphis that your great-grandfather knew. Stagecoaches rumbled along the dusty road from Nashville, mail traveled yet in saddle bags. The glamorous Mississippi River steamboat was just beginning to come 'round the bend, for that romantic era was still in its infancy. Eli Whitney's cotton gin was paving the Old South's road to riches; everywhere the great cotton plantations were gnawing deeper into the wilderness, a new culture of ease and elegance was arising and the foundations of great fortunes were being laid in a region only recently won from the Indians.

For a more detailed picture of the times, let us glance at Keating's History of Memphis:

"The period between 1840 and 1850 was for Memphis a remarkable one. In that time her population grew from 1799 to 8841; her first great Commercial Convention was held; the Memphis & Charleston, her first railroad, was chartered; the Gayoso House was built; a theater was established here and, of more importance still, The Memphis Appeal was founded on the ashes of The Western World.

"The Shelby County Bible Society was organized, a weekly stagecoach and mail line to Charleston, S. C., was established, a military road to Little Rock and a canal from Wolf River (to turn the water wheels supplying power for prospective Memphis industries) were agitated."

It was an era when young Memphians were shooting squirrels in the grove of trees where the Hotel Gayoso now stands, when the mayor of the little city drew a salary of $500 a year (he was not paid at all until 1841), when two nightwatchmen with lanterns policed the town, when river water was hauled up the levee in barrels three times a week for the city's chief water supply, when "driving faster than a trot" was punishable by a $10 fine, when horse thieves and other evildoers were locked up in the little brick "calaboose" that stood in Market Square.

But the roots of The Commercial Appeal's history are buried even deeper than a hundred years ago.

For seven years after Memphis was laid out in 1819 by Andrew Jackson, John Overton and James Winchester, it had no newspaper. At the close of 1826, when the population numbered about 500 souls and a charter of incorporation had been obtained, the proprietors of the town decided to start a newspaper. The result of this effort was the importation of a few cases of type and a Washington hand-press by steamboat from Cincinnati and the birth of The Memphis Advocate and Western District Intelligencer under the editorship of one Tom Phoebus in January, 1827. Despite its lengthy name the paper was a small four-page sheet, devoted largely to boosting the sale of town lots in Memphis and supporting the political aspirations of Gen. Andrew Jackson.

Early in 1832 T. Woods & Co. started The Western Times and Memphis Commercial Advertiser. Soon afterward the two papers were consolidated and in 1835 this combination succumbed to The Memphis Gazette which had been started in 1834 by P. G. Gaines, an intense partisan of President Jackson.

The Gazette expired in 1838 and in January, 1839, Dr. Solon Borland started The Western World and Memphis Banner of the Constitution. In 1840 this newspaper was purchased by Col. Henry Van Pelt and in the same year its name was changed to The Memphis Appeal.

Thus began the story of a journalistic institution that for 100 years has survived the tragedy of Civil War and yellow fever, the vicissitudes of panic and the march of time. It sprang from a hardy stalk, for the early history of Memphis reveals few characters more interesting than Dr. Solon Borland and Col. Henry Van Pelt.

Dr. Borland was born in Virginia in a day when George Washington was still alive, and Colonel Van Pelt traced his Dutch ancestry to the early settlers of New Amsterdam, as he had been born in New York state.

Dr. Borland was a member of the town's first medical society and his marriage in 1839 at Calvary Episcopal Church was a social event of early Memphis. After selling his newspaper to Colonel Van Pelt he moved to Arkansas, was a major in Col. Archibald Yell's regiment in the Mexican War and, in 1848, succeeded Ambrose H. Sevier as United States senator from Arkansas. At the outbreak of the Civil War he returned to Memphis and became a brigadier-general in the Confederate Army and died in Houston, Texas, in 1863.

Coming to Tennessee in pioneer days, Colonel Van Pelt began his editorial career at Franklin, a few miles south of Nashville

From 1840 until his death in 1851 he edited The Memphis Appeal. He is now but a handful of forgotten dust in old Winchester Cemetery, recently converted into a children's playground, but the imprint and the impress that he made upon his city and his community still endure after a hundred years.

Thus was The Commercial Appeal born—and a century of Southern journalism begun.

Long before the War Between the States, the paper that is today The Commercial Appeal was an "oldtimer" in the MidSouth it served.

CHAPTER II

"Befo' De Wah"

TODAY the mighty, block-long presses of The Commercial Appeal sing their song of succeeding editions as the news-wet papers cascade forth at the rate of over 125,000 daily and 150,000 on Sundays. The wires of its far-flung news services spread like a huge spiderweb over the face of the civilized world, telephoto machines transmit important pictures with the speed of lightning, 300 regional correspondents are on duty in cities, villages and hamlets in the MidSouth, more than a score of reporters gather the local news and dozens of editors fight deadlines as they write headlines.

It is a far cry, indeed, from the days of 1840 when Col. Henry Van Pelt, The Appeal's first editor, got out the paper almost alone in his little frame office that stood on the muddy banks of Wolf River.

Newspaper facilities and equipment in those days were as primitive as the times, which saw four-horse stagecoaches rumbling in from Nashville in the foggy dust of Old Raleigh Road and hundreds of flatboats, laden with upcountry wares and produce, tied up at the Memphis wharf. Only a few years before a flatboat from the Illinois River had coiled its line over a tree stump at Colonel "Wappanooo" Ferguson's Arkansas plantation just opposite Memphis and a tall and lanky young flatboatman had gone ashore and earned a few honest dollars by chopping cordwood. The young flatboatman's name was Abraham Lincoln.

Colonel Van Pelt's mechanical equipment consisted of a few cases of type and the old Washington hand-press that he had inherited from The Western World and Memphis Banner of the Constitution. As the telegraph was still an inventor's crazy dream, his "news service" consisted of newspapers from New Orleans, Pittsburgh, Cincinnati and Louisville that kindly steamboat captains and mates brought to him. To facilitate matters, Colonel Van Pelt nailed an "Appeal Box" to a post at the river landing, in which the steamboat men could leave the papers when he was not on hand to greet them.

Editor Van Pelt's nimble shears and ready paste pot did the rest and, all in all, he was able to turn out a pretty good newspaper—although sometimes the news was several weeks late. But even then there were difficulties; witness this item from The Appeal of Aug. 12, 1845: "In consequence of the low stage of the water we have no late mails from up the river. This is particularly vexatious at this time, as the elections in Missouri, Indiana and Kentucky have taken place during the past week. We fear that the earliest news from these places will be by the stagecoach from Nashville."

The newspapers left in the editor's box at the river landing were gratefully acknowledged in the columns of The Appeal. Typical was the following item published about that time: "Thanks to the splendid Steamer James Robb for the Louisville papers from which we obtained much news." But not always were these favors so fruitful of results for witness this notice, illustrative of the extreme candor and politeness of the day, that appeared on Dec. 27, 1844: "We are indebted to the clerk of the Steamer Uncle Sam for the late New Orleans papers. We thank him very much, but there is nothing of interest therein."

In 1841 The Memphis Appeal turned its column rules in mourning as it published the first "big story" in its history—the death of President William Henry Harrison, the first president to die in office. He was a 68-year-old veteran of the War of 1812, who, because he wanted to wave at the pretty girls, disregarded his physicians' warning not to ride horseback in his inaugural parade on a cold, blustery day in March, 1841, and expired of pneumonia in the White House a short time later.

Similarly did The Memphis Appeal turn its column rules in mourning when its great political idol, Andrew Jackson, died at the Hermitage in 1845—and so impressed was the editor with the importance of the story that he threw all the advertisements for coffins, bearskins and pills and patent medicines, etc., off Page 1 and published a news item there for the first time. It was a daring journalistic innovation but progressive Editor Henry Van Pelt did not hesitate to set a precedent.

The feeble, flickering fame that had been the life of the famed "Old Hickory" went out in a great bedroom at the Hermitage late on a Sunday afternoon, but it was not until the following Thursday that the news, traveling in the saddle bags of a galloping mail rider, reached Memphis.

Here is the story of General Jackson's death as The Memphis Appeal published it on June 14, 1845:

"A GREAT MAN HAS FALLEN! GEN. ANDREW JACKSON, the Hero, the Patriot, the Sage—He Who 'Has Filled The Measure of His Country's Glory' Is No More!

"Information to be relied upon was received here on Thursday evening from Nashville, conveying the painful intelligence of the demise of this truly great and wonderful man; he departed from this life at the Hermitage at 6 o'clock on the evening of the last Sabbath, aged 78 years in March, last. We have delayed the publication of this paper until as late an hour as we possibly could, in expectation of the arrival of the Nashville mail with particulars, but are compelled to go to press without them or to postpone furnishing our distant subscribers with their paper until the next mail.

"P. S.—The Nashville mail is in and the papers of that city only contain a mere confirmation of the fact of the death of General Jackson, as their papers were put to press in a few hours after his death."

The next few days brought more news of the grim old hero's passing . . . "he is represented to have retained his faculties to the end and to have died at 6 p.m. on Sunday, the 8th inst., quietly, calmly and with entire resignation amidst the beloved members of his family and a few intimate friends who were present." It was also recorded that in Memphis a public mass meeting of sorrow was held at the Commercial Hotel upon call of Mayor Finley and that Editor Van Pelt presented the resolutions of mourning on "the melancholy event," the said resolutions being adopted "by the assemblage of a large and respectable number of our citizens."

Time and events continued their swift pace. The next year, 1846, the Mexican War broke out and The Appeal chronicled the departure of Memphis' volunteers under Capt. E. F. Ruth (an employe of The Appeal) for the front, by steamboat via New

Orleans. From Vicksburg there drifted back the news that one of the volunteers had shot and killed another in a quarrel arising from a serious breach of etiquette on the part of the latter—he had failed to tip his hat to a lady. Hot words followed and horse-pistols flamed.

The news-pregnant year of 1849 brought the California Gold Rush that sent numerous Memphians, like thousands of others, trekking across the Western plains and deserts as they braved both thirst and Indians in their desperate zeal to claw sudden riches from Mother Sierra's chest of hidden treasures. Again, The Memphis Appeal was there to tell the story in the language of the day. The news, traveling by prairie schooner, was long in coming but on Dec. 14, 1850, The Appeal was able to publish a letter written by a Capt. W. W. Gift to Editor Van Pelt which told how the Memphians were faring. One of them, Jesse D. Carr, was reported to have struck it rich in a sandy creek bed and scooped out a fortune of $200,000.

Meanwhile, The Memphis Appeal, a success from the start, was growing fast under Colonel Van Pelt's aggressive leadership. It had begun as a four-column weekly, subscription rate $3 a year, but by July 30, 1844, it had developed to a semiweekly and raised its price to $5 a year.

The change to a semiweekly came simultaneously with The Appeal's vigorous support of James K. Polk, a Tennessean, for the presidency. "It is hardly necessary," wrote Editor Van Pelt in announcing the new edition, "to remind our Democratic friends that by appearing more frequently the usefulness of The Appeal in a partisan point of view is greatly enhanced."

The Appeal was intensely Democratic. Editor Van Pelt rejoiced mightily at the defeat of Henry Clay in 1844, for Henry Clay was a Whig, and to a good Democrat a Whig was as reprehensible as a horse thief. This intense partisanship extended to the news columns as well—witness this report of the appearance here in 1844 of a distinguished speaker: "John J. Crittenden, the Kentucky big gun of Whiggery, spoke in Court Square Tuesday. We were not present, but we think very little of his effort."

Not even a disastrous fire that swept The Appeal's new plant over Browning's grocery at Poplar and Main on Feb. 27, 1845, could retard its surging progress and its steady growth and on Sept. 9, 1847, the little triweekly paper, recently changed from a semiweekly, blossomed forth as a daily.

Within a remarkably few years, Colonel Van Pelt had firmly established The Appeal and had become the most famous editor in all the Western country. To his journalistic ability was added the asset of an outstanding personality, for he was a man who looked the important role that he played in his community.

As big in stature as in mentality, he towered more than six feet in height beneath his tall beaver hat and weighed more than 200 pounds. There was something about his face that held one's attention—the gentle, but firm, mouth; the dimpled, almost boyish chin; the intellectual forehead, the fine brow and eyes, the dignified sideburns and the finely shaped head with the quaint style of wearing the hair that was cut long in the manner of the times. Along with all this, his eloquent, old-style broadcloth attire, high collar and padded stock stamped him as a gentleman above the ordinary.

For nearly 10 years, Henry Van Pelt continued to put out his fast-growing newspaper with the aid of the journals supplied by friendly steamboat captains and his ready paste pot and shears, and then the epochal happened. The telegraph came.

For several years Samuel Morse had been tinkering with his mysterious "electric telegraph" that he had patented in 1840, the same year The Appeal was born. Now he had succeeded in making the thing work; messages actually had been sent between Washington and Baltimore with the speed of lightning's flash. Improvements had been made and now a thin network of copper wires was beginning to connect the cities of the East and to creep toward the South and the West.

In May, 1848, Memphis tapped the Nashville-to-New Orleans telegraph line at Tuscumbia, Ala., and on the morning of May 23 Editor Henry Van Pelt—ever alert to progress—printed in his Memphis Appeal the first telegraphic dispatch ever given to newspaper readers in this city. It was about the Democratic National Convention at Baltimore, and it began:

"BALTIMORE, Md., May 22.—The opening session of the Democratic Convention on Monday elected Andrew Stevenson of Virginia president, and several vice presidents and secretaries. The committee reported on all the delegations favorably, except those from New York . . ."

By June 1, The Appeal was printing cotton quotations from New York and river stages from Pittsburgh within a few hours after they had been recorded. No longer was it compelled to

THE DAILY APPEAL.

"Mon Dieu et Mon Droit,"

SATURDAY MORNING, MARCH 15, 1851.

FOR GOVERNOR,
GEN. WILLIAM TROUSDALE.

The Concert.

Well, the Ninghtingale has come, has caroled and flown. Barnum has made seven thousand dollars by the operation, and the good citizens of Memphis are left to their criticisms, to compare notes, and ascertain if possible, the important fact, we ther they have received a quid pro quo; or in other words, whether they have been benefitted to the amount of the price paid for their tickets. Others who hold money at less value, are left to the interesting and philosophical speculation as to whether there is any thing in Jenny's singing really calculated to run the world mad. All will readily admit that she possesses great vocal powers, probably greater than any other living female, certainly greater than any it has ever been our good fortune to hear. But the knowledge and admission of this fact do not meet the difficulty and solve the mystery to what it is that has so enraptured and charm the human race. Others have sung as swee and with as much, probably more pathos, if with such compass and volume, though we sure none ever have commanded the vocali which she is complete mistress, with less ing effort. It is this, in our judgment, constitutes the principal charm in her s The clear and dulcet strains well up, as it wer voluntarialy from the soul, and are poured forth upon the auditory with a power as captivating as it is irresistible. But the secret charm that captivates the heart is not found alone in this. While we may *admire* the song, we can but *love* the songstress. Possessing a mild and placid ntenance, lit up by an occasional smile, she ms the very personificati odness, with nce fo rularly re-

Rail Road

The time has pass and the plains,—the the dead level cour tages of Railroad en Rail Road Engine has tion which is the resu and investigation, by J Hosel, Virginia, that an ascent in the road mile. A letter from Ric Sun, thus f the "The vhic made is m tion of to sills are c n wit rail six e and up e, ext inc n una w s ten in a These of the d n in a ese w com us tantl u de he

wer of two ing te

Mr. Elizur W lately res discharge he

When Jenny Lind sang in Memphis in 1851, under the management of P. T. Barnum, The Appeal told the story in these words. She is shown in the inset.

wait upon steamboats, stagecoaches and galloping post riders for its news of the outside world.

In the MidSouth, from which the Indians had been removed less than a generation before, a new agricultural empire of infinite promise was being carved out of the wilderness as the cotton fields advanced and the dark forests and tangled canebrakes retreated. The need for adequate transportation for a growing section was fast developing, and once again The Memphis Appeal was there to tell the story in the language of the day and hold aloft the guiding torch of progress.

As early as 1840, the year The Appeal was founded, the glamorous steamboat era that was to make the Mississippi a river of romance for 50 years was born in Memphis when Editor Van Pelt encouraged the owners of several independent steamboats to merge into two Memphis companies, one serving the St. Louis-Memphis-New Orleans trade and the other the Louisville-Memphis-New Orleans trade. The latter was named "The Lightning Line," because its big sidewheelers made the trip from Memphis to Louisville in the incredibly fast time of five days.

With the coming of the steamboats, the flatboats that had drifted lazily down to New Orleans with their cargoes, faded from the river. Cotton now rolled down to the sea at a fast pace, bales stacked high on broad decks and smoke trailing from tall iron stacks in feathery plumes. Beneath the crystal chandeliers in the elegant salons of these floating palaces, the whale-oil lamps cast their soft glow on life and gaiety—ladies in silks and satins, gentlemen in broadcloth and fancy waistcoats.*

Prosperity had come to an area that had been an Indian wilderness only a generation before, fabulous fortunes were being built in King Cotton's new empire as the planters waxed rich. But a big need remained—and Editor Henry Van Pelt mulled over it as he sat in his editorial sanctum. That need was a railroad, for cotton was still being hauled to the river landings by ox team, a slow method at best and an impossible one when rainy weather turned the narrow roads into streaks of hub-deep mud.

Already primitive railroads were spreading their shiny iron fingers over the East, and Editor Van Pelt and others saw in this area both the need and the opportunity. And so, as the result of their efforts, the first railroad that Memphis ever saw —The Memphis & LaGrange—was built.

A shiny little engine with an upright boiler and tall smokestack ("it looked like a coffee pot on wheels," said someone) and

* For steamboat disaster that killed Mark Twain's brother, see Page 1, Appendix.

a few high-wheeled, rattly cars with bench seats were brought by steamboat from Cincinnati. And so, on May 6, 1842, The Memphis Appeal was able to announce:

> "MEMPHIS & LA GRANGE RAILROAD—The Memphis & LaGrange Railroad has been completed six miles out. Cars leave every afternoon at 3 o'clock, returning in time for supper. Fare, 50 cents. Cheap enough, truly."

But the little railroad never reached its projected destination of LaGrange, Tenn., by which it could have tapped the big cotton plantations. Six miles out it ran into an insurmountable obstacle in the form of Col. Eppy White, who owned a 4000-acre plantation near what is now White Station. Hefty Colonel Eppy —who weighed well over 200 pounds, and who had once bet Davy Crockett a barrel of whisky that he could make a bigger splash by jumping into Wolf River than Crockett could—was adamant. He wasn't going to have that snorting little firebox running over his plantation and scaring the daylights out of his cows! No, sir!

And so Memphis' first railroad died a-borning. The tiny train ran six-mile pleasure trips for adventure-loving Memphians for a while, then the novelty wore off and the sheriff finally caught up with the shiny little locomotive and sold it for debt.

Although Memphis' first railroad died the movement lived, and it not only lived but it grew. In 1845 The Appeal was instrumental in bringing about the historic Commercial Convention in Memphis, at which John C. Calhoun presided and to which came 700 of the South's most distinguished men to plan railroads, highways, levees and many other improvements for a section that only recently had been an Indian wilderness.

Out of this grew the plans for the Memphis & Charleston Railroad—and in 1857 came the "iron horse" to wed the Mississippi Valley and the Atlantic Seaboard with bands of steel. The two-day celebration that featured the opening of this railroad on May 1 and 2, 1857, was a landmark in Memphis' history. Thousands paraded under the great arch of gas lights erected at Main and Madison, a barrel of water from the Atlantic Ocean was brought to Memphis and ceremoniously poured into the Mississippi River to symbolize the uniting of the two, Court Square reverberated with the thundering speeches of orators who saw the dawn of a new era for Memphis and its golden future as the great metropolis of the mighty valley.

The headlines in the yellowed old files of The Memphis Appeal of May 2 and 3, 1857, breathe the story:

"THE GREAT RAILROAD JUBILEE OF YESTERDAY!!! . . . Thirty Thousand People In Council! . . . South Carolina, North Carolina, Georgia, Mississippi and Tennessee Cement Their Union! . . . Imposing Procession of Volunteer Firemen, Councilmen and Citizens! . . . Eloquent Speaking and Immense Enthusiasm!"

"SECOND DAY OF THE GREAT RAILROAD JUBILEE!!! . . . The Mingling of the Waters! . . . The Atlantic Ocean and the Mississippi River Are Now As One! . . . The Space-Annihilating Locomotive Comes! . . . The Multitude Cheers!"

The new era had arrived. No longer was it necessary for travelers bound for eastern cities to take a steamboat to Cairo and board the railroad there. The stagecoach lines cut their rates. The new railroad proudly advertised in The Appeal that Nashville was only 25 hours away, connections being made at Stevenson, Ala. Even New York City was only four days and five nights from Memphis in the wake of the wood-burning locomotives of the Memphis & Charleston.

The South—the rich, romantic Old South of Yesterday with its ease and elegance and its leisure and its luxury—had come into its own and Memphis, with its railroad, was the queen city of the fertile Mississippi Valley.

But Col. Henry Van Pelt did not live to enjoy the triumph for which his paper had labored. In 1851, death halted his career in the midst of his editorial labors. He was buried in old Winchester Cemetery beneath a tombstone that read merely: "H. V. P., Editor of The Appeal. Died April 23, 1851."

Long ago that faded monument crumbled to dust, but in its place has come a new monument to Henry Van Pelt which has endured through the years . . . The Commercial Appeal that is today "The South's Greatest Newspaper."

With the Civil War and the fall of Memphis began the romantic odyssey of The Appeal, unmatched in the annals of American journalism.

CHAPTER III

"The Greatest Rebel of Them All"

IN ALL the hundred-year-old history of The Commercial Appeal, there is no more romantic chapter than the story of this newspaper's three years of wandering over the South after it had been driven from Memphis when the city fell to the Yankees in the Civil War.

From the outset of that bitter internecine conflict in April, 1861, The Appeal had been such a strong advocate of Southern rights that Southerners had praised it as "the voice of the Confederacy" and Northerners had assailed it as "the hornet's nest of the rebellion." It was certainly the former and very likely the latter for, in the light of those flaming times, The Memphis Appeal was unquestionably "the greatest rebel of them all."

Intensely Southern in its sympathies, The Appeal had, as early as 1858, printed in full the historic debates between Lincoln and Douglas and, in 1860, it had supported Douglas in his unsuccessful campaign for the presidency. When South Carolina went out of the Union, the first state to do so, The Appeal worked up a big torchlight procession in celebration of the event. When the Confederate States of America were formed and Jefferson Davis was inaugurated as president at Montgomery, The Appeal came out with an editorial entitled "The Birth of A New Nation," a masterpiece of fire and eloquence that will live as long as the English language remains a living tongue.*

* See Page III, Appendix.

In April, 1861, the war that The Appeal had predicted since the day that President Lincoln was inaugurated in March crashed against the pages of history and the pages of The Appeal as well. Fort Sumter, in Charleston harbor, had been fired upon, blood had been shed . . . and here is the headline that Memphians read in their paper on the morning of April 13, 1861:

> "THE CIVIL WAR BEGUN! . . . The Conflict Inaugurated at Charleston! . . . The Fire Returned by Anderson! . . . A Breach Effected by the Charleston Batteries! . . . Two of the Sumter Guns Silenced! . . . Base Treachery of Lincoln's Administration Disclosed! . . . Triumph of the Southern Forces Probable!"

The Appeal kept up its editorial campaign for Southern rights and in June, Tennessee—last to withdraw—followed the other Southern states out of the Union. For a few days Tennessee was a state without a Nation, and then it threw its lot with the Confederacy. The die was cast.

War news literally raced through The Appeal's columns, as the yellowed old files show. A recruiting office for the Confederate Army was opened in the Gayoso House. Volunteers began swarming to the colors, bringing their own rifles and pistols and horses for the Confederate Army as yet had little equipment. The Memphis & Charleston Railroad shops were hastily converted for the manufacture of cannon and the casting of solid iron balls. Men were drilling and parading on every downtown street and the air was thick with the blare of bugles and the ruffle of drums.

The Appeal's stories of General Lee's smashing victories in Virginia fanned the eagerness of every man between the ages of 16 and 60 . . . hurry . . . hurry and get there before the war was over and it would be too late! Confederate flags began to flutter over Main Street buildings and the editor of The Appeal, in an elaborate ceremony, was presented with a silken flag by the ladies of Memphis. The paper recruited and sent to the Confederate Army an artillery battery bearing its own name.*

In November the war came home to Memphis. The city's volunteers clashed with the Yankees in their first battle at Columbus, Ky., and 400 to 500 were reported killed. The dread headline in The Memphis Appeal of Friday morning, Nov. 8, 1861, told the story that gave the war a different color.

* See "The Appeal Battery," Page V, Appendix.

"BLOODY BATTLE AT COLUMBUS! . . . Victory Claimed By The Confederates! . . . The Enemy In Full Retreat! . . . Terrible Slaughter On Both Sides! . . . Memphis Troops Engaged! . . . General Grant Reported Killed!" . . . so the headline read.

All that day crowds waited in the streets outside The Appeal office for the names of the dead and wounded to come trickling over the lone telegraph wire from The Appeal's correspondent on the battlefield . . . anxious wives, weeping mothers, grim-faced fathers of the men and boys at the front. "What's the news?" was the question on every trembling lip, asked in a tone that mingled both hope and dread.

But no casualty list came that day and to a city whose heart was torn by wild anxiety for loved ones, The Appeal was compelled to announce in an editorial the following morning:

"The city of Memphis had some 3000 combatants in the army up the river and scarcely was there a human being amid our vast population of 40,000 persons who did not have a brother, father, husband or at least a friend among them. The extent of our information is contained in the brief, but portentious announcement that 'our loss was heavy' and anxious minds could learn no more."

That day, however, the eagerly-awaited news began to filter over the wires, bringing happiness to some and grief to others. So-and-so was safe, so-and-so was dead, so-and-so was badly wounded. The suspense that had gripped the tense throng now dissolved into smiles of happiness or tears of sorrow.

In a few days the wounded were brought home on a steamboat that landed at the foot of Jefferson Avenue. Tender hands carried them to wagons, fitted with mattresses and featherbeds, which took them to a hotel on Main Street which had been hurriedly fitted up as a hospital. There they were nursed by that noble band of women known as the Southern Mothers.

The war raged on. Fort Henry fell, Fort Donelson fell, Fort Pillow fell as the invading Yankees crept closer. And in April came the Battle of Shiloh, barely 100 miles from Memphis, the bloodiest engagement ever fought on the American continent up to its time as thousands died.

The Memphis Appeal's sympathies for the South were no keener than its enterprise, for it was represented at the Battle of Shiloh by its own staff correspondent, a man named Ette, and his story stands today as an epic of journalism. On the

The start of the Civil War was our biggest story in 1861. The illustration, showing the firing on Fort Sumter, is from the old files of Harper's Weekly of that year.

blood-soaked day of April 7, 1862, as Ette scribbled his story amid the thunder of the cannon and the scream of the shells, he began his story like this:

Special to The Memphis Appeal

"BATTLEFIELD, April 7—We slept last night in the enemy's camp ... "

Eight words told the story of the first day's battle, a story that present-day writers might expand into columns and still tell less.

But the next day's news brought dark tidings of disaster. The Yankees had brought up reinforcements, the tables had been turned. The heroic Gen. Albert Sidney Johnston, idol of every Memphian, had been killed—shot as he galloped forward on his horse in a dashing charge, waving with his sword for his men to follow him. The bloody engagement was over, the battered Confederates had retreated to Corinth, Miss., and the Yankees, and their dead, were in possession of the field.

The Confederate defeat at Shiloh made the fall of Memphis inevitable. On the morning of June 6, 1862, Memphis was captured by the Yankees after a battle between Federal and Confederate gunboats in the harbor, and with the city's fall there began a story that has no counterpart in American journalism.

The defiant Memphis Appeal, after declaring editorially that it would sink its presses to the bottom of the Mississippi River rather than surrender to the hated foe, loaded its equipment into a box car and became a homeless wanderer over the Southland. For three years it was a roving exile, dwelling wherever the fates of war made it necessary for it to be but continuing to publish. Successively, it was issued at Grenada, Miss., Jackson, Meridian, Atlanta and Montgomery, as it boldly and defiantly retained its masthead of "The Memphis Appeal."

Publishers of the paper then were Col. John R. McClanahan and Col. Benjamin F. Dill, who had become owners after the death of Col. Henry Van Pelt in 1851. They lacked none of the journalistic fire that their predecessor had displayed, and it was their efforts that made The Memphis Appeal the most conspicuous champion of the Southern Confederacy.

As early as April 29, 1862, when the fall of Memphis seemed certain, The Appeal had announced its decision in an editorial. It said:

"The Appeal will continue to be issued punctually in Memphis as long as the city is in possession of the Confederate authorities. Should it, however, be occupied by the enemy, taking a lesson from the despotic suppression of the Nashville journals by Andrew Johnson, we shall discontinue its publication here and remove to some point in Mississippi where we can express our political sentiments and still breathe the pure and untainted air of Southern freedom.

"We cannot do such violence to our feelings as to submit to censorship of Lincoln's hireling minions that would deprive us of the privilege of expressing at all times our earnest God-speed to the process of Southern independence and the right to write and speak what we think. Sooner would we sink our types, press and establishment into the bottom of the Mississippi River and become wandering exiles from our homes."

This fiery challenge to the Yankees was no idle gesture, for The Appeal meant what it said. Early on the morning of June 6, while Federal and Confederate gunboats were thundering in Memphis' harbor and ramming each other with their ironclad snouts, Colonels McClanahan and Dill, Composing Room Foreman S. C. Toof and Pressman Andy Harmon loaded the paper's equipment in a box car and started South.

At Grenada, 100 miles from Memphis, The Appeal halted and there publication was resumed three days later.

The lead story that day told of the capture of Memphis, under this now-historic headline:

"THE FALL OF MEMPHIS! . . . Naval Battle On The Mississippi! . . . Destruction of the Confederate Fleet! . . . Escape of General Van Dorn With $200,000 Worth of Property! . . . The Federals In the City! . . . Events Of The Day, Etc."

Explained an editorial in the same issue:

"TO OUR READERS—The occupation of Memphis by the Federal forces has convinced us of the necessity for removing our offices to Grenada, Miss. In taking this step, our principal motive has been to continue in a position wherein we may be able to render official service to the Cause we advocate, hereafter as heretofore, and in accomplishing this, should we succeed, we will find our greatest reward.

"Our fate is indissolubly connected with that of the Confederacy. Our political action in the past has been well understood. We cannot desert the one or change as to the other. Our political ideas were not formed to be cast aside under any exigency that can possibly happen; and so long as two or three states are gathered together in the name of the Confederate States, so long will we be found advocating, as zealously as ever, a continued resistance to the tyranny which a haughty foe is endeavoring to establish over us. . . . We have an abiding faith in the success of the South."

But even in those dark days of bitterness, exile and sorrow, The Appeal never lost its sense of honor. Witness this editorial:

"POISON AND THE DAGGER? NEVER!—It is with regret we have, in two or three instances, seen expressions in Southern newspapers speaking of poison and the dagger as a means of ridding the Confederacy of some of her most odious and prominent enemies.

"Of course, such expressions have been rare and were the result of feelings momentarily excited and overwrought; but however obscurely hinted and palliated with whatever provocation they may be, any declaration in favor of the cowardly act of assassination must be met with stern and indignant rebuke.

"The Southerner deals in no secret stab; quick to resent insult and maintain his personal honor, he looks his enemy in the face and meets, breast to breast, the open foe. Our men will give their blows in the light of day on the open field and history, whatever it may have to record of their success or their failure, will be compelled to register in everlasting characters, that in the time of sharpest trials the Southerner's deeds were honorable and his character unsullied.

"While honor remains, all is not lost."

If this sense of honor ever faltered or if The Appeal's faith in the South's cause ever waned, there is not a line in the faded old files to show it. In the momentous three and one-half years that followed there were days, trying days, when The Appeal's pressman had to use shoe blacking because the paper couldn't get ink (the smudgy old files breathe the story) and when there appeared to be imminent necessity of having to print on wall paper because it was almost impossible to get any other kind. But the faith that can move mountains can likewise overcome obstacles, and The Appeal continued to publish.

Do you wonder why The Memphis Appeal was called "the Bible of the Confederacy" and why it was read so eagerly by the gray-clad soldiers around their campfires in the Confederate camps? If so, read a stirring editorial on the occasion of a Confederate victory by Gen. Stonewall Jackson which follows.

"The star of the victorious Jackson is again in the ascendant and once more he is pushing forward after an utterly defeated and flying foe. General Jackson's motto is the correct one—fight the enemy wherever you can find him, and if he will not offer you battle, go after him and compel him to fight.

"Give us a little more of these tactics and the war will soon assume a much more favorable aspect. The Federals can be forced to abandon our states and our cities, our people can return to their homes in peace, and the Confederacy will take her place among the nations of the earth."

But despite stout hearts and dauntless courage, the Yankees came on, as the defiant Memphis Appeal continued to fan the flames of Southern resistance.

"Let them at every advance they make meet with a deadly volley from every thicket," thundered an editorial on June 19, 1862, as the Federals approached Holly Springs, Miss. "Every rifle and shotgun in the country should be brought into requisition and the Federal soldier should be taught that every step they make further into the South is made with hazard to themselves. Even in the absence of our army, it is within the power of citizens to harass, terrify and hold the enemy at bay."

The Appeal's advice was followed. Southern planters put the torch to their cotton and the conquering Yankees found only ashes where they had expected riches. Apropos, The Appeal remarked: "A people determined to be free will submit to any sacrifice and cannot be conquered!"

The fighting had now begun at Vicksburg and the enemy's river boats were opening fire "from a safe distance," we read on June 20. McClelland had been brought to a stand before Richmond, and The Appeal believed "the fortunes of war have turned in our favor and we will finally achieve our independence."

Time rolled on, July opened with McClelland in full retreat and Yankee shells whining over Vicksburg in steadily increasing numbers, and both armies girding for the approaching battle. "The Success of Our Arms" was the caption of a defiant editorial.

Times in Memphis were growing more troublesome, The Appeal reported through a correspondent in the city who seemed to be operating right under the noses of the Yankee commanders, smuggling out his dispatches each day. The captive city had greeted the conquering foe with sullen defiance. Ministers who prayed for the Confederacy were suspended and otherwise "effectively admonished." Families of all persons holding commissions in the Confederate Army or who had volunteered therein were banished from the city, as were the families of persons who had been active for the Southern cause. No man who refused to take the oath of allegiance to the Federal Government could engage in business or practice his profession. And worst of all, The Appeal lamented, the Yankees had taken possession of its plant and were publishing a Yankee newspaper from it. "To what base uses we have come!" The Appeal mourned at this sacrilege.

The Irving Block on Second Street overlooking Court Square had been converted into a military prison, and in it a number of Memphis' leading citizens were confined, amid conditions of indescribable squalor and filth. One of the prisoners was Mrs. Matthew C. Gallaway, wife of Memphis' Confederate postmaster; she had smuggled out letters to Southern friends beneath the folds of her hoopskirt.

So many Confederate families were being banished from the city that The Appeal offered its services as a clearing house for their letters. "No matter where you go in your exile," The Appeal said, "you can write your friends in care of our office at Grenada and they can do the same." The letters were forwarded promptly and scattered friends reunited—for everybody read The Appeal.

It was difficult for the paper to get news from the North in those trying days, since the enemy's lines had cut off all communication in that direction, but the editors of The Appeal were not nonplussed. They published a request that "gentlemen who arrive from the United States with late papers, will please leave them at the editor's room, over George Lake's store, next door north of the Collins House." The editor added: "In these days of uncertain mail from the South and a blockade from the North, our facilities to furnish the news from all quarters can be greatly increased by a little attention on the part of our friends."

Still the war rolled on, still Confederate reverses came, but still The Memphis Appeal continued to breathe the spirit of Southern defiance. "Now, By St. George, The Work Goes Bravely On!" was the caption of an optimistic editorial following the news of the August victories in East Tennessee.

Winter came and with it the problem of warm clothing for the men in the Confederate trenches. The Appeal urged "the loyal daughters of the South" to get busy at once with their "spinning wheels and hand looms and knitting needles." And the response, as The Appeal said a few days later, "demonstrates the unconquerable patriotism of our mothers and daughters who are solidly behind our brave men in the field."

But despite grim resistance and bloody fighting, Grant and his invading Federals crept closer toward Grenada. November found the little city practically surrounded by the enemy, all supplies cut off and The Appeal, in the absence of ink, printing its pages with boot blacking obtained from the Confederate Army's commissary stores.

By Nov. 29, Grenada's fall was inevitable, and on that day —after printing a farewell edition with the latest news of the Yankees' approach—The Appeal loaded its press and equipment on a railroad car and departed . . . this time for Jackson, Miss.

The homeless "Bible of the Confederacy" had resumed its wanderings over the Southland whose cause it championed. Before it lay two more years of bitter trial, sacrifice and hardship . . . and also Meridian, Miss., Atlanta, Montgomery and the final crushing of its hopes in the little town of Columbus, Ga.

Shelled out of Jackson, Miss., by Grant's thundering guns, The Memphis Appeal — homeless but still defiant — continued its wanderings.

CHAPTER IV

A Homeless Wanderer

"THOUGH driven from home, we are not among strangers," wrote the editor of The Memphis Appeal in December, 1862, when, after having been chased out of Memphis and Grenada by the advancing Federals, his wandering journal unloaded its single-cylinder press from a box car and came to rest at Jackson, Miss.

Little did this editor realize, however, that Journey's End was not yet; that in less than six months "The Voice of the Confederacy," which had taunted and defied the Yankees at every turn, would be routed from Jackson, Yankee shells screaming over the heads of its crew as they fled across Pearl River in a flatboat with their precious press.

But let's continue that editorial, which appeared on Dec. 13, 1862, the day The Memphis Appeal began publication in Jackson.

"The Appeal has ever met a generous welcome and received a cordial support at the hands of the people of Mississippi, and so long as we are privileged to remain within her borders we shall feel that we are among friends and brethren," it said.

"Hoping that we have been and may yet be of some service to the state, we have a desire verging upon ambition to keep our paper alive during the war. By dint of our own energy and the blessings of good fortune we have thus far been able to keep in advance of the enemy's lines, and would fain hope that we have now made our last retrograde move.

"Should the enemy permit us to remain in our present location until wild war's deadly blast is blown and until gentle peace shall have assumed her benignant sway over the land, we shall rejoice at the sacrifices we have made in keeping our offices out of the clutches of the enemy."

And so, in the South's fast-darkening days of the Civil War, the peripatetic Memphis Appeal took refuge among its friends and neighbors at Jackson, Miss. Its office was on State Street, a few doors below the postoffice, and there it resumed its labors for the Cause for which it was willing to stand or fall.

Editors McClanahan and Dill unpacked their editorial pens and took them in hand, keen-edged journalistic sabers ready for fresh battles with the enemy. Composing Room Foreman S. C. Toof set up his type cases, ready to mold words into eloquent bullets of lead. Pressman Andy Harmon erected his clicking, one-cylinder press—the weapon that would discharge these bullets of defiance and send them hurtling against the foe.

These were trying times, for newspaper materials of every kind were scarce. A shortage of paper made it imperative for The Appeal to reduce its size to six columns, and substitute nonpareil type for eight-point in order to crowd in more words. But courage lived for . . . "we now have an agent at the paper mill in Georgia and hope, in a short time, to be enabled to greet our readers again on a sheet of the usual size."

A feeling of pathos tinged with admiration for dauntless hearts comes as one turns the crackling pages of the yellowed old files that mirror those historic days.

On Christmas Eve, 1862, comes the news that Holly Springs has been captured. Not a word about the holiday season. Only the grim news of battles, the names of men who yesterday were alive and virile and who are today maimed or dead.

On Christmas Day the paper is issued as usual. Still not one word of Christmas, not even an indirect reference to the festival or a single advertisement of Christmas goods. Men's thoughts were on other things, for the pinching necessity of the times left neither opportunity nor desire for holiday celebration.

The old year passes, the new year dawns but there is no mention of this except a stirring editorial on the progress of the war. It begins: "The new year breaks upon us with cheering beams of hope and promise. Our arms are successful, our troops in the main are in high health and spirits, while the enemy is reported disheartened and despondent."

On Jan. 8 appears a notice that The Appeal would like to make arrangements for "a supply of good, dry wood." It is needed to fire the boiler that turns the single-cylinder press.

On Jan. 17 appears an advertisement by M. Stern & Co., indignantly denying a report that flour sold by them is mixed with sand. These gentlemen assert that the only foundation for this damaging rumor is the fact that they are selling flour at $65 a barrel, whereas other dealers are charging $80. Good coffee is advertised at $3.75 a pound, other things in proportion.

The food problem is fast becoming graver. For the approaching planting season, The Appeal urges the farmers to plant but little cotton and much grain. There is a double reason for this, the editor explains; it will supply food so badly needed at home and prevent the Yankees from getting their hands on cotton for which their idle New England mills are clamoring.

Things are looking darker at Vicksburg. Fifty Yankee transports and three more gunboats have arrived and the firing is getting hotter. Folks down the river say the distant rumble of cannon can be heard almost every day now.

Forrest is giving the Yankees hell in Tennessee, raiding deep into their territory with his hard-riding cavalry, blowing up their ammunition dumps and capturing rich stores from their wagon trains. Good old Forrest; more food and blankets and clothing for hungry and ragged Confederates.

And so runs the news of those momentous days when the South's future was being fashioned in the mold of war.

On Jan. 31, 1863, after having for six weeks appeared as a newspaper of varying shapes and sizes because Pressman Andy Harmon used whatever paper he could get his hands on, The Appeal received a supply of regulation paper and resumed its eight-column form. At the same time, it discarded the tiny type that had been made necessary by the lack of space.

Refugees from Memphis were still arriving in Jackson, bringing with them stories of how the residents of the city were outwitting their Yankee captors. Malaria had struck heavily in the Confederate lines south of Memphis the previous Summer and no precious quinine was available. One day a Yankee sergeant found a dead mule on North Main Street and ordered several negroes to drag it outside the city limits. The negroes did, whereupon waiting Confederates ripped open the dead mule's sewed-up belly and removed a big supply of quinine that Confederate friends had hidden therein. A lot of Confederate soldiers quickly got well of malaria.

As in Grenada, The Appeal's office in Jackson was a clearing house for the letters of exiled Southerners whose families had been scattered to the four winds. Letters came, the names were published and soon they were forwarded—for every Southerner in the area read The Appeal. Printed, too, were advertisements about missing families. A typical advertisement, on March 10, notified a Mr. J. B. Elam that he could find his family at the Pearce House, in Canton, Miss.

Prices of everything were high and going higher. Letter paper was reported to be selling at $5 a quire in Shreveport, whereupon the editor of The Appeal observed caustically that "enough of this article ought to be impressed to write the seller's passport to—well, the other side of the River Jordan."

Whisky sold at $2.50 a drink, "and the barkeep does the measuring." Strawberries were offered at $2 a quart—"forbidden fruit to us," said the editor.

Vicksburg was now threatened by land and by river, as Grant continued to tighten his noose around the Confederacy's Gibraltar in the Mississippi Valley. Firing was heard every day now, and it was realized that the next 60 days would be pregnant with events. Mississippi was going through her most trying ordeal of the war. Yankee forces were marauding over the state. Fire followed sword as the invader came on, and mounds of smouldering ashes stood today where great old Southern mansions stood yesterday. Sherman was proving his own statement.

On every side the grim picture darkened, but The Memphis Appeal, as defiant as ever, called in burning language for "every man in the state to rise and drive out the hated foe!"

By order of President Jefferson Davis, March 27 was observed as a day of fasting and prayer for the Confederacy— with no intended irony toward a people who had fasted so long and prayed so often.

May opened with a Yankee raid toward Jackson and the Great Northern Railroad, interrupting communication with the South, and equally ominous was the news that firing had been heard along the Yazoo. More stories said that Confederate soldiers were hungry for food, and crying out in an editorial headed

"Once More to the Breach!" The Appeal called upon Mississippi's women and children to "feed such men as are within your reach."

By May 4, the air of Jackson was electric with rumors of the most exciting kind. Crowds milled before The Appeal office, tense for the latest news of the foe's relentless advance; wagons and cotton drays and even buggies were being hurriedly loaded with household equipment as residents prepared to flee—to where, they did not know.

The Appeal pleaded for calmness as it decried a panic—but at the same time it kept a weather eye on Grant's relentless advance from the west as, with a great encircling motion, Grant laid his trap for doomed Vicksburg. The Appeal was calm, but one who was calm could also be careful.

The Yankees came on, the sharp Federal raids drew nearer and nearer to Jackson and the low rumble of the big guns could be heard in the distance, ominous heralds of impending doom. At last even the final star of hope faded from the darkening sky, and nothing remained but courage.

In this grim hour, when the Yankees were battering at the very doors of Jackson, The Appeal promised its readers that it "would continue to publish until the evening and morning of the last day of probable security."

And The Appeal kept its word. It continued to issue editions until the morning of May 14, 1863, when it was shelled out of Jackson by Grant's booming guns. Grant and Sherman, to whom The Appeal had long been a journalistic thorn of the sharpest kind, were certain they were about to bag The Appeal at last as their scouts had furnished them with a copy of that morning's issue, fresh and damp from the press. But all they got for their hopes was a defiant editorial, taunting them for their failure to capture the paper.

But let The Appeal's war-time pressman, Andy Harmon, tell of that historic flight when The Appeal crossed Pearl River, Yankee shells dropping around it. Harmon is dead now but here's what he said when a reporter interviewed him in 1890 on his recollections of that momentous day:

"We got all packed up and ready to go. Myself and Bassett, who was then foreman of the composing room, were the rear guard. We crossed Pearl River in a flat with our mules, and had just made the trip when the Bluecoats reached the other bank. They had nothing to cross on so they took it out in cussing us, and we gave 'em back as good as they sent. There's a heap of men who feel mighty brave when they've got a big river between them and the other fellows. We cut loose the flat and she went sailing down to the Gulf. They cussed us some more and we mounted our mules and rode to Brandon, Miss., where all our truck had been carried."

As the Yankees entered Jackson from one direction, The Memphis Appeal went out in the other, full 40 rounds of shot and shell making a pother over its head before it could get out of the way of those two military commanders whose pride had been wounded by its cool taunts. One can imagine the chagrin of Grant and Sherman when they reached out to grab The Appeal —and drew back a derisive editorial.

The clicking one-cylinder press with its wood-burning boiler that had toiled so heroically in Memphis, Grenada and Jackson, now went on to Atlanta, but the small proof press and a few cases of type were taken to Meridian, Miss., where The Appeal set up shop and issued "extras" in the size of handbills for a week.

In his capture of Jackson, Grant had made his famous move from Bruinsburg by which he had isolated General Pemberton and shut him up in Vicksburg, to be bagged in that starving city on the Fourth of July after the historic 46-day siege that cut off the town from the outside world and reduced soldiers and civilians alike to a diet of mule meat. General Grant had captured "the Gibraltar of the Confederacy," but he had failed to capture the Confederacy's voice and its most fiery champion.

Memphis had fallen. Vicksburg was doomed. New Orleans had fallen. From Cairo to the Gulf, the Mississippi Valley was in the hands of the enemy. But a citadel of the Confederacy's hopes was still safe in Southern hands—Atlanta. And so, gathering its type and its press and what little else of the world's goods it possessed, The Memphis Appeal went there.

And Generals Grant and Sherman doubtless bit their lips.

Sherman's exploding shells were tearing craters in Atlanta's streets when the last of The Appeal's crew fled that besieged Dixie city.

CHAPTER V

Atlanta—And Sherman

IT WAS just one year to the day after the capture of Memphis by the Yankees that The Appeal, a homeless wanderer over the war-torn Southland, began publication in Atlanta.

In making its bow there on June 6, 1863, the paper said: "In casting its lot with the people of Georgia, The Memphis Appeal will refrain from all interference in the domestic affairs and dissensions of the state. To the Confederacy we owe our first great duty, and when we have faithfully performed that duty we shall have accomplished the object of our highest ambition."

In describing The Appeal's flight from Jackson, Miss., the editors mentioned with evident enjoyment the fact that one of the first acts of the Yankees in Jackson "was to inquire as to our whereabouts, and they were not slow at expressing their rage at our escape. We flatter ourselves our evacuation was a masterly one—and it was accomplished without loss, notwithstanding a number of shots were fired across Pearl River at our rear guard by the disappointed Yankees."

Once in Atlanta, the correspondent and reporting forces were enlarged, and arrangements made for publishing full and reliable information—an accomplishment, no doubt, upon which some large orders for job printing for the Confederate Army had an important bearing. All paid subscribers were notified that the time lost in the removal from Jackson to Atlanta would be added to their subscriptions.

Atlanta then was a city of feverish activity. Here, the Confederate Government had set up foundries for the casting of cannon, machine shops, arsenals, armories and factories for the manufacture of ammunition. Day and night the hammers clanged and the sparks flew, and the sickening smell of saltpeter from the powder mills hung over the city like a pall. As General Sherman had told General Grant, "the capture of Atlanta would spell the deathknell of the Confederacy."

Food was scarce and prices were high, hundreds of sick and wounded Confederate soldiers filled the military hospitals set up in schools and churches where they were nursed by hoop-skirted Southern women, but despite all the privations and horrors of war, there were nevertheless some very pleasant days in Atlanta. The Appeal's office was situated on muddy Whitehall Street, between Decatur and the Atlanta & West Point Railroad, and it soon became a favorite gathering place of many men who were famous in the annals of the Old South.

Among these were Albert Roberts, erstwhile editor of the Chattanooga Rebel, which had fled down to Marietta, and young Henry Watterson, then managing editor of the Atlanta Confederacy, and later of the Louisville Courier-Journal. Like Colonels Dill and McClanahan of The Memphis Appeal, they were journalistic exiles, and as such they had something in common.

There was too much war activity to admit of dullness, and the hard and constant work left no time for repining, even had there been any inclination to do such. The course of events that were shaping history was closely followed; each victory of the Southern arms brought exultation, no defeat was allowed to pass without some consolatory view of the situation.

When the Yankee blockade cut off the supply of printing ink, shoe blacking was again used. Again there were times when the paper supply ran low that Pressman Andy Harmon considered printing The Appeal on wall paper, but this necessity never arose as, fortunately, the blockade was evaded and the paper came through.

News was hard to get. Telegraph facilities were meager at best, and often when important dispatches were expected from the front the wires were down—perhaps at the hands of a raiding party that was burning the railroads and blowing up the bridges.

To make matters worse, it was hard to get wood to fire the boiler that drove the clicking one-cylinder press.

But things that could not be cured were philosophically endured, and The Memphis Appeal struggled on. "Dixie's" newsy letters from Richmond continued to give The Appeal's readers bright and crisp reports of the current activities in that sector. "Shadow's" letters from Chattanooga, now an important seat of the war as the Yankees fought their way southward, kept the readers posted on the battles and movements in that major area.

As the war wore on, prices of necessities which had been high now became almost astronomical. The South's most fertile regions had been desolated by the absence of its men in the army, and scarcity existed in every crop that fed man or beast. The blockade was so stringent as to practically cut off the outer world, and such things as medicines and coffee were almost forgotten, except for the success of an occasional smuggler whose prices were fabulous.

Bacon was $3 a pound; lard $2.10; butter $4; sugar $5—and these prices quoted in The Memphis Appeal of 1863 were by no means the climax.

The invading Federals had freed the negro slaves that came within their scope and enrolled many of them in their army, to fight against the South. The South's railroad system was so run down and shattered as to be incapable of transporting supplies promptly. The ragged Confederate Armies were meeting reverses in the field, strongholds were being captured, territory divided, prisoners held without exchange.

But the South held grimly on—and so did The Memphis Appeal, driven far from home but still within the land whose fortunes and whose fate it had accepted as its own.

Early in the year there had been hope, but now hope itself was beginning to fade. In swift succession came the disaster to Confederate arms at Gettysburg, the loss of Port Hudson, the success of the Yankees at Charleston, the falling back of General Bragg at Chattanooga, and Sherman's thrust toward Atlanta, the citadel of a dying cause, where he hoped to break the backbone of the Confederacy.

On the seventh of July, in accordance with a proclamation of Governor Brown, business was suspended throughout the state of Georgia and the people of every locality met and organized for home defense. The young men had gone to the army, but old men and young boys shouldered shotguns and squirrel rifles and prepared to resist the invading foe. In calling upon the people to take every possible step, The Appeal tersely said: "We must either drive the Yankees out of our country or be overrun and robbed by them."

Was there bravery in Southern hearts in those dark days? Let these lines from an editorial in The Appeal of July, 1863, answer for themselves:

"Let us not court despair, but summon courage and with 'Nil Desperandum' as our motto, and a merciful and just God to guide us, we shall evoke victory from the cannon's mouth!"

The grim picture grows darker, but the South hangs on.

Lee retreats from Pennsylvania, the flower of his army crushed at Gettysburg, and under the caption of "Never Despond! Never Despair!" The Appeal publishes an editorial beginning: "True manhood and heroic courage never despair, but rise superior to the calamities that befall them. . . ." Then follows an effort to show how many stars of hope and encouragement are shining through the dark clouds of gloom, and once more calling upon the South to rally against the foe.

Elsewhere in the Confederacy there was talk of surrender, but if there was any such sentiment in Atlanta The Appeal did not reflect it. Rather, the case was the obverse, for on the last day of July The Appeal published an editorial under the caption "No Cause For Despondency" which counseled the careful handling of resources and declared the South might have ample cause to hope for ultimate success. "He who fights in a righteous cause is doubly armed," The Appeal said.

The Appeal never lost courage or surrendered the faith, and yet, with an honesty that even burning emotion could not sway, it refused to create false impressions. More than one strong editorial was directed against "those who are humbugging themselves and others by belittling the numbers of the enemy," as the editor cautioned "Let us not be humbugged; to be forewarned with the truth is to be forearmed with the power for the deed."

Came December, 1863, and with it The Memphis Appeal's second Christmas in exile. There was no joy, no celebration—only an editorial of sympathy for the waifs of war, an appeal for remembering "the numberless mothers who are now widowed and the little boys and girls who are without fire and without shoes on their naked feet on this day."

Copies of The Memphis Appeal issued at Atlanta and Montgomery during the paper's Civil War exile show that it boldly retained its name, despite the change in datelines. Here are two issues of that historic era.

With this tiny one-cylinder press (top), which was moved from city to city in a box car, The Appeal fought the Civil War. The page, from an issue of 1872, shows the new press (below) which was substituted in that year for the old one.

Pathetically, another editorial in the same issue recalled Christmas customs and family reunions that the South had known in the happy days before the war, and concluded: "And though many of us may be absent from home, in the army, in the hospitals and elsewhere, let home, with its images of father or mother, or brother, or sister—with its memories, its hopes, its joys—be intellectually as though actually present; and let the reunion of heart and mind be as complete as though we were not absent in the body."

On Jan. 28 The Appeal editorially rebuked some ladies of Atlanta for having made the rounds of the city soliciting contributions for a carpet for the parsonage of one of the local churches. "In times like these," The Appeal said, "when numbers of our soldiers are suffering for covering to shield them from the chilling blasts of Winter, and their families at home are suffering for the actual necessaries of life, such action is not only condemnable but reprehensible. If any of our ministers have carpets on their floors it is their duty to convert them into blankets and send them to the army. Let us hope that these no doubt well-intentioned ladies will think better of their enterprise." Apparently The Appeal's rebuke caused the good ladies to abandon their plan as the old files mention it no more.

Times in Atlanta were getting worse, and, as The Appeal said, "people's faces have grown so long the barbers charge a dollar for a shave." But all was not jest. Quinine was $200 an ounce, the butchers had put the price of beef up to $3 a pound, and bacon was equally as dear. Granulated sugar was $10 a pound, potatoes $12 a bushel, soap $4 a pound, butter $10 to $15 a pound, and candles $5.25 a pound. Clothing and hats were just as high—"a love of a bonnet" was advertised for $1000.

But Sherman's blue-coated hosts came on through North Georgia as Johnston's gray ghosts, reduced to hunger and rags, continued to fight and fall back . . . fight and fall back . . . fight and fall back. For dreary days and weary miles, they fought and fell back . . . fought and fell back.

Came May and the Yankees were at Dalton. Came June and the winds from the north brought the low rumble of distant cannon from Kenesaw Mountain. Closer and closer the enemy came until June 24, when The Appeal announced "an important movement which we cannot mention has taken place." Press reports ceased, all wires being cut as the Yankees drew still nearer to Atlanta. Came the 27th and 28th of June, and loud firing was heard to the north of the city.

Then came Sherman—and the end.

A few hours after The Memphis Appeal published its issue of June 30, 1864, Yankee shells began falling in the city, tearing craters in the streets, and the siege of Atlanta was on. The Appeal loaded its press and equipment in a box car and fled from the Georgia capital. But it continued to issue a small paper on its proof press for the benefit of the ragged Confederates in the rifle pits defending the city until Atlanta fell on Sept. 2.

As General Somebody's corps marched into Atlanta on one side, The Memphis Appeal hurried out of town on the other side, the smoke from the burning munitions plants being blown up by the retreating Confederates shrouding its withdrawal.

Sherman had won his victory and a ruined city, but he had failed to bag The Memphis Appeal—the same paper that he said afterward, in his memoirs, was "the last newspaper to leave Atlanta."

Once more "The Voice of the Confederacy," its head bloody but still unbowed, was a homeless wanderer in a war-torn land. But Montgomery, Ala., was yet a stronghold of the Confederacy, so The Memphis Appeal went there.

The Yankees caught up with The Appeal at last, arrested its editor and scattered its type in the street. Later, the weary homecoming.

CHAPTER VI

Journey's End

THE CONFEDERACY'S sun was slowly setting, and its day was nearly done when The Memphis Appeal, driven out of Atlanta by General Sherman's famous march to the sea, resumed publication in Montgomery, Ala., in September, 1864.

Sherman, from whom The Appeal had escaped at Atlanta only in the nick of time, continued to carve his path through Georgia with fire and sword, pausing here and there to smash the presses of Rebel newspapers and scatter their type in the streets. But as yet, he had not succeeded in laying hands on "the greatest rebel of them all," to use the words by which The Memphis Appeal was still acclaimed by the Southerners and assailed by the Yankees.

As the black clouds of the South's disaster deepened it must have seemed apparent to Colonels McClanahan and Dill, editors of The Appeal, that such a fate awaited their beloved journal which had eluded and taunted the enemy for more than three years. They were right, for early in 1865 the Yankees caught up with The Appeal at Columbus, Ga., and captured it. Journey's End had come at last.

But that's getting ahead of our story—

Arriving in Montgomery in September, 1864, with its one-cylinder press and a few cases of type, The Memphis Appeal set up an office in a little frame building just across the muddy street from Montgomery's Exchange Hotel. Now, like the South that was also making its last stand, it had come to "the cradle of the Confederacy" and its busy little press whirred only a few blocks from the state capitol with its tall stone columns where Jefferson Davis had taken the oath of President of the Confederate States of America a little more than three years before.

The price of the paper was raised to 50 cents a copy. In Atlanta less than a year before the price had been only 25 cents. But the increase was not surprising in view of the fact that during the past year the price of a barrel of flour had risen from $100 to $300, and a pound of butter from $3.50 to $8. Currently, Montgomery's banks were offering $5000 of Confederate money for $100 in gold.

The news was as dark as the times. The Yankee Armies were gaining everywhere, as the ragged Confederate forces were beaten back. General Lee, in a message to his soldiers published in The Appeal, told them that theirs was the choice between renewed fighting and abject surrender as he added: "To such a proposal brave men with arms in their hands can have but one answer."

The news from abroad was equally dismal. It was clear now that England's Queen Victoria, of whom the South had hoped much in return for its cotton that her long-idle mills in Lancastershire so badly needed, would do nothing.

The pall grows deeper as Autumn comes and harvest time finds ruined fields bare of food for either man or beast. Christmas arrives, but instead of being a season of joy it is only a bitter reminder of the happy days that were. The New Year dawns, but its only cheer is that it cannot possibly be worse than the year that has just died.

But the South holds on. And so does The Memphis Appeal as it mirrors for history the last days of the Confederacy. Let us glimpse that picture as we turn the brittle pages of the yellowed old files.

It is Sunday morning, March 5, 1865, and the ill-starred Confederacy is rapidly crumbling to the ruin that fate has decreed will envelop it with Lee's surrender at Appomattox on April 12, less than a month later. Pressman Andy Harmon mounts his stand, the little one-cylinder press begins its clickity-click and The Appeal comes out as usual.

The news that it tells is as grim as the times it reflects.

"The fall of Charleston is now confirmed," says a dispatch, "and Stanton claims the fall of Wilmington. A victory obtained by Lee over Grant, on the 23rd inst., is reported from Washington, but it would seem that the dispatches of the 24th did not confirm it, or else the reporter would have alluded to it. We have strong hopes, however, that it is true, for it is possible that later dispatches were suppressed by the Federals at Memphis."

And this:

"The New York Tribune's correspondent says: 'It is estimated that the capture of Charleston and Fort Anderson, with certain capture of Mobile, will liberate 25,000 men from the Federal Navy who can be put into the Federal Army.'"

And this:

"NEWS FROM ABROAD—The report of Queen Victoria's speech at the opening of Parliament shows that the South need not expect anything of England. British humanity has not as yet sickened to the bloodshed in America."

Three and one-half columns of fine, solid type are given to the report of General Joseph E. Johnston, issued at Vineville, Ga., on Oct. 20, 1864 (the news seems to have been a long time in coming), in which the general explains why he failed to save Atlanta from the Federals the previous Summer.

A statement signed by General Lee announces that all Confederate deserters who return to their commands within 21 days will be granted pardons. The plea obviously implies that many disheartened men have quit the hopeless fight against overwhelming odds and gone back to their homes and farms.

As if seeking to instill new courage into disheartened soldiers, a Confederate poet who signs himself "I. G." contributes an inspiring verse under the title of "The Soldier and the Croaker." Three stanzas, typical of the dozen others, read:

> *It is a time, my corpulent friend,*
>   *When the foes are thund'ring around—*
> *And our duty is now to defend,*
>   *To the last, each foot of ground.*
>
> *By the widow's moan—by the orphan's tear—*
>   *By the shrieks of the helpless maids—*
> *By the burning homesteads far and near,*
>   *That mark their cowardly raids.*
>
> *I swear I'll fight, if I live I'll fight!*
>   *Those hellish hordes forever—*
> *But bend the knee or surrender the right?*
>   *Never—never—never!*

But the South's days of fighting against overwhelming odds were near an end, and so were the days of The Memphis Appeal whose romantic odyssey had begun three years before.

Major General James H. Wilson with his 9000 Spencer rifles in the hands of picked men who knew how to ride and shoot, came on through Alabama. He gobbled up Selma, burning foundries and factories, and everything else that bore the "C. S. A." brand of ownership. By early April he was almost within sight of Montgomery, and immediate evacuation of the city became necessary.

Again The Memphis Appeal's clickity little press took wings of steam, and this time it fled across the Chattahoochie River to Columbus, Ga. But the flight proved futile; Montgomery was occupied on April 12, 1865, without resistance, and Columbus captured on April 16, after a stout but ineffectual defense. The battle was fought after Lee's surrender, so poor were the communication facilities.

One of General Wilson's first acts was to seize the equipment of The Memphis Appeal which had taunted the Yankees for nearly four years, smash all its machinery that he could find and scatter its type in Columbus' streets. But, fortunately, The Appeal's historic press had been smuggled out of town two days before and was now safely hidden from Federal eyes at Macon, Ga. Thus it escaped capture.

Col. John R. McClanahan, senior editor of The Appeal, made good his get-away but Col. B. F. Dill, his junior associate, delayed his departure on account of the illness of his wife and was captured by Federal soldiers. After some search, Dill was found by Col. Minty and conducted to General Wilson's headquarters at the Perry House.

When the editor and his captor entered General Wilson's room, the Yankee commander was seated on the floor with his engineer officer, a large military map spread out before them.

"Allow me," said Col. Minty, with a triumphant smile, "to introduce to you, sir, Col. Benjamin F. Dill, editor of The Memphis Appeal."

The Yankee general jumped to his feet, electric with excitement. "Have we caught that old fox at last?" he fairly shouted, "Well, I'll be damned!"

There was a good laugh and a gentlemanly handshaking all all around, followed by some choice old Bourbon which Colonel Dill declared to be better than any he had tasted in two years.

General Wilson gave Colonel Dill the choice of posting a bond of $100,000 not to publish The Appeal any more for the duration of war, or being held a prisoner. Dill promptly gave the bond and was released.

The story of the last days of The Appeal as a wanderer over the war-seared Southland was told by Andy Harmon, its Civil War pressman, in an interview that a reporter for the paper obtained from him in 1890, nearly 30 years after the conflict. Mr. Harmon, then an old man, was a railroad crossing watchman in South Memphis.

"General Wilson's cavalry wound us up at Columbus, Ga.," he said. "They burned and broke up all the plant except the Hoe press and the boilers and engine which had been hidden in Macon.

"McClanahan and Dill, the owners, and Dumble, one of the editors, were there with us. McClanahan and Dumble saved their bacon, but the Yanks captured Dill and his wife next day and brought them back. They took all the good money the Dills had, a lot of silver in dimes and quarters, and they likewise got Dill's hat. It was a genuine wool hat, and Dill set great store by it. Mrs. Dill came to me, crying, and said: 'Oh, Mr. Harmon, the Yankees haven't left us a thing!' 'Same here, ma'am,' I says. I felt mighty sorry for her. You see, the Yanks had likewise nailed me and Hedges and Bill Brisbin and a few more of our crowd."

Andy Harmon paused, sucked his stubby pipe reflectively, blew a thick cloud of smoke and went on.

"Myself and Hedges and Brisbin were paroled and went on down to Mobile. From there we went across to New Orleans on a boat. Hedges was acquainted with the barkeeper and he fixed us up for passage and all the drinks we wanted. At New Orleans, I got transportation back to Memphis through Mr. Sinnot, one of the editors of the New Orleans Times."

Toward the last, Harmon said, the printers were being paid 75 cents per thousand ems and his own salary as pressman was $75 a week. But salaries were offset by the higher cost of living, for he paid as much as $5 each for his meals.

"And tough grub? Well, I'd rather not talk about it," the veteran pressman laughed. "There wasn't enough food in that country to feed a cat. Coffee was $18 a pound, eggs $5 a dozen, and meat—mostly liver and things like that—$5 a pound. Whisky was never less than $2.50 a drink, and the rockiest stuff you ever went up against; it simply made callouses in your throat. It wasn't easy to get, either.

"After a while, I found one of our negro firemen whom we had brought from Memphis was a pretty good cook so I and Hedges and one or two more who slept in the office, put the negro on commissary duty. The rest of the boys, however, sometimes went as empty as a drum. Of course, Dill and the other big bugs boarded at the hotel and got the best there was to be had.

"But speaking of that darkey, he was the biggest rascal and the best forager the world ever saw. He could steal a chicken or a side of meat if there were a dozen men standing guard over it with fixed bayonets. Nothing was too little and nothing was too big for him to tackle. His name was Dave and he belonged to John A. Denie, the Front Street lime merchant."

Old Andy Harmon puffed his pipe again and grinned expansively as the blue smoke curled from his white beard.

"What d'ye think that darkey did at Columbus?" he asked. "Stole a whole barrel of whisky from the hospital stores and then stole a mule and a dray to cart it away, and drove around to our headquarters with the plunder. It was just before the Yanks entered the town and, of course, we wouldn't refuse anything that came to hand, knowing it would be captured and burned when they got in. Them hospital stores was under heavy guard and how Dave got away with that stuff will never be known until Judgment Day.

"The Yanks almost captured our likker, but we were too quick for them. We took the barrel from the first place we had stored it and hid it in another place and covered it with trash. Bye and bye, here come a lot of Yanks. They went to the place where the barrel had first been put, but of course they didn't find it. Lucky for us they didn't poke their bayonets under that trash."

After another reflective puff on his pipe, Harmon resumed, telling about the departure from Columbus.

"As soon as the coast was clear, we went and opened the barrel and filled all the bottles and jugs we could carry and put out across the Chattahoochie River. We didn't want any transportation as long as the stuff lasted. There were five of us in the party, myself and Good, Hedges and Brisbin and a Yank named Bill Fields, of St. Louis, who had strayed off from his company.

"When we got started, Good says: 'Look-a-here, boys, we ain't taking anything along to eat.' 'Eat, hell," says Brisbin, 'look at all the whisky we got!' And Bill Fields, who was loaded to the guards by this time, speaks up and says: 'I move we make that noble sentiment unanimous!' And so we did, being by that time the owners of the earth.

"It was a good thing we adopted that Yank. When we got to Montgomery he told the other Yanks of the friendship we'd shown him, and they treated us like white folks. It was easy then for myself, Hedges and Brisbin to get our paroles and our transportation down to Mobile, from where I went to New Orleans and then took the steamboat back to Memphis."

The end of the four-year Civil War had come at last, and, for the time at least, "The Memphis-Grenada-Jackson-Meridian-Montgomery-Columbus Appeal," as the soldiers in the Confederate armies jocularly called their old friend, was no more. It had gone down with the Lost Cause, whose fate and its future it has accepted as its own and for which it had fought as bravely as any Confederate soldier on the gory battlefields.

Behind The Memphis Appeal lay the greatest romance in the history of American journalism. Before it lay the weary return from exile, re-establishment of the paper in Memphis and resumption of its faithful service to its city and its community which has continued down to this good day.

The Civil War was over at last, and in 1865 The Appeal came home, resuming publication here on Sunday morning, Nov. 5.

CHAPTER VII

The Road Back

THE Civil War was ended, the ill-starred Confederacy was a smoking ruin, the South lay desolate in its ashes of defeat and the romantic journeyings of The Memphis Appeal—its equipment smashed and its type scattered over the streets by Yankee soldiers at Columbus, Ga.—were over at last.

It had done yeoman service for the Southern cause. Hardly a soldier of the Western armies but knew it as an old friend, a welcome visitor around his camp fires and one that held the torch of the Confederacy on high as it brought news of home and loved ones to the mud-caked rifle pits. It had been more than a newspaper; it had been something with a heart, a soul.

During all its wanderings—Grenada, Jackson, Meridian, Atlanta, Montgomery, Columbus—it had boldly kept its title, "The Memphis Appeal." Here it had been founded and here it had dwelled for 20 years before the outbreak of the conflict, and some day, when the fates of war decreed its exile at an end, it was coming home.

In November, 1865, The Memphis Appeal did come home.

The journey was a long and arduous one. It required months as the weary trail led through the South's burned cities and past its desolate fields. Ruin lay on every hand. The flower of the South's young manhood was in the hospital or the grave. Great family fortunes had crumbled, and poverty was widespread. The freeing of the slaves had destroyed the only social and economic system the South had ever known; a new system would have to be built. Behind lay the war, but ahead lay an even greater task—reconstruction.

And so The Memphis Appeal, which had fought the war as bravely as any Confederate soldier with a gun, came home to help rebuild the city and the region whose story was its own.

The one-cylinder Hoe press that had escaped the Yankees when all other equipment was destroyed at Columbus, Ga., was taken from its hiding place at Macon, Ga., and hauled to the Tennessee River in a cotton wagon. There it was placed aboard a steamboat and started on its way down to the Mississippi River, and back to Memphis.

At Cairo, the faithful little press unloaded at the river landing while its penniless editor cast about for means to get it aboard a steamboat bound for Memphis. The task proved easy, for The Memphis Appeal had been a friend of Mississippi River steamboat captains for 25 years. A friendly captain gave free passage to both editor and press, and in due time they arrived in Memphis.

By some means that history does not disclose, money was obtained for the purchase of more type and equipment. Soon, Memphis was placarded with the following announcement:

"Having, after many vicissitudes of the late Civil War, returned home, The Memphis Appeal will present itself as a candidate for the favor of the reading people of the South, and the states of the Mississippi Valley. As heretofore, it will endeavor to deserve public confidence everywhere as a reliable source of public information.

"It can offer to the people with whom it has sojourned during the past three years no better guaranty than its past endurances, that, in the future as in the past, their interests and welfare will form the leading object of its solicitude and efforts."

On Sunday morning, Nov. 5, 1865, The Appeal's return from Elba was consummated as the little one-cylinder press began clicking again and the first issue appeared.

An editorial, prominently displayed, explained:

"If The Appeal erred in obeying the impulse that throbbed as from one impassioned heart throughout the South, it may claim to have some expiation in the sacrifices it has endured during its three years of self-exile.

"We have no unmanly excuses to make, no stultifying recantation of opinions once honestly entertained, but the stern logic of events has practically compelled their renunciation. We frankly and truly accept the interpretation that has been stamped with the red verdict of war on the Constitution, of the indestructibility of the Union of States and people which makes us, for all time, a mighty and indivisible Republic. We recognize and abide by the logical sequence of the late, unhappy Civil War in the destruction, now and forever, of the institution of African slavery.

"The real men of the land, the true fighting soldiers of both sections, have decreed that there shall be a real peace and a genuine union in our great American family. Between the veteran Federal soldier and the unflinching Confederate soldier, who have so often met each other in the conflict of battle, there is a respect which affords the sure foundation on which the restored Union will rest."

And so, offering no apologies for the past, but turning its eyes to the future, The Memphis Appeal took "The Road Back."

When the first copy flipped from the clicking little press, Maj. Will O. Woodson, one of The Appeal's employes, seized it and ran to a room at the Gayoso House where Col. B. F. Dill, the editor, lay ill. Major Woodson dashed into the sick room, waving the paper over his head.

Mrs. Dill seized the paper and kissed it passionately, as though it was a thing of flesh and blood. Then she spread it affectionately over the bed of her pale, sick husband. To her, it was an emblem of all the hopes and the struggles and the failures of the "Lost Cause" for which it had labored so heroically and for which it had sacrificed so heavily.

But Colonel Dill looked at things more practically. He raised himself on his pillow, picked up the paper and began hunting for typographical errors. Though a sick man, he was still an editor.

It would be pleasing to think that after all their bitter trials, the two famed Civil War editors of The Appeal—Colonel Dill and Colonel McClanahan—could settle down to a long career of peace and prosperity. Such was not to be. In the Summer of 1865, a few months before publication was resumed, Colonel McClanahan fell from a window at the Gayoso House and was killed. Colonel Dill lived to see the re-establishment of the paper in November, but he passed away the following January. A public funeral which hundreds of Memphians attended was held for him at the Gayoso.

The return of The Appeal to Memphis was the subject of much comment by the Nation's press—both North and South—and many stories were carried, describing the paper's romantic odyssey. One of these was the Cincinnati Commercial, in which appeared an editorial under the caption of "A Wanderer Returns."

Wrote this Yankee editor:

"During the war the frequent removals of The Memphis Appeal caused a great deal of merriment, and journalists especially kept an account of its wanderings and amused themselves at its expense. The paragraphs on the subject have been innumerable, and it is doubtful whether the proprietors of The Appeal were always able to see where the laugh came in.

"We received many copies of The Appeal when it was issued at Grenada, Jackson and Atlanta, and the ample extracts from its columns that may be found reproduced in the Cincinnati Commercial are the best testimony we can offer that we recognized The Appeal as a good newspaper.

"We remember well the copy of The Appeal issued at Atlanta on the morning of the Battle of Peachtree Creek. It was full of fight, and we should not be surprised if the headlong valor of Hood's Army that day was due, in no small degree, to the fiery appeals addressed to the men to make their fight then and there. . . "

So much for the Yankee comment; now for the other side. An excellent example is found in the Nashville Banner of 1865, written by Albert Roberts, himself a "traveling journalist" in war days, first with the Chattanooga Rebel and then with the Atlanta Confederacy, and a frequent visitor at The Appeal's office in Atlanta.

Prophesying that "a hundred years from now The Appeal's story will read like a romance," Southerner Albert Roberts wrote:

"Do our eyes deceive us? No, it is The Memphis Appeal which stares us in the face! The same old letter, Roman bold, at the head; the same antique decorations and plain captions; the very ink, as it were, the very paper!

"We stand, so to say, in our own shadow and read it like a page of 'Waverly.' Esto perpetua! Here is the portly and impressive Dill, like a burgher of the olden time, in broad-brimmed hat and silver-headed cane, just as he used to pass from Whitehall to Peachtree, undismayed by the shells; unmoved by the dreadful stench of saltpeter; here, hovering in the air, is the bleeding form of poor McClanahan; and here, dripping with water and wrapped with moss, is the brilliant but ill-fated Linebaugh who was drowned during one of The Appeal's many flights.

"The history of this journal will read a hundred years hence like a romance. It has had more adventures than a Knight of Malta, and has come out of the smoke and din covered with scars but stronger and braver for the conflict. It has heard lions roar and seen the sea puffed up with winds; its haps and chances by flood and field make matter for a ballad. Nothing in newspaperography can compare with its strange, eventful career.

"Ah, that old press! How well we remember it! Clickity-click! Clickity-click! Clickity-click! Through the long night it rattled away, defiant of the storm outside; and every morning how bright and fiery, how unfatigued and fresh it looked, like a war-horse ready for another charge.

"They carried the works on Peachtree Creek. They carried the works below Decatur; they carried the rifle pits that ran along the road to Macon. Clickity-click! Clickity-click! The old press dashed along heedless of danger, a living cognizant being, cast of iron, steel and melt.

"Dill grew serious; Dumble's face extended, and McClanahan's pen wandered vaguely across the page. Old Joe Johnston was down the country and Hood was playing the devil. Then Stonewall Jackson was gobbled. There was a pause, an ominous lull. The bloody 22nd of July was past, the bloody 28th had been lost, and Ben Hill knew no more about Sherman than he did about Paradise; Hood, like Dill, was serious, and the boys at the front were serious. Hardee was off at Jonesboro. Boom! Boom! Boom! How the guns thundered! Crash! Crash! How the roofs and the church spires tumbled! Whiz! Whiz! How the shrapnels tore through the air! Clickity-click! Clickity-click!

"Atlanta fell. Out we went, like the snuff of a candle, and darkness followed. It lasted long; it was thick with fog—unstudded with stars. Linebaugh lies at the bottom of the Alabama. McClanahan, God rest him, sleeps on the banks of the Mississippi. Day begins to break. Clickity-click! The old press is going again with the gallant Dill upon the flat.

"It is all over now. It seems like a dream. What shadows we pursue. May our ancient friend never be shadowless; but may it bear the sun to mark its shadow.

"Here's to your health, oh Dill! May you never move again, oh, Appeal, except your readers!"

It was barely a month after these lines were written that Colonel Dill joined Colonel McClanahan in death. Although neither of these two brave editors long survived the episode, they did succeed in their ambition to keep their paper alive throughout the war. In death, they joined a brave companion—Linebaugh, a fluent and brilliant writer who had been drowned while the fugitive Appeal was crossing the Alabama River on its last flight. An ex-clergyman of the Episcopal Church, very erratic but full of fine traits of character, he had joined The Appeal's staff in Atlanta and was loved like a brother by the two exiles.

The Memphis Appeal was back home, its romantic Civil War saga was at an end. But that was 75 years ago—and its usefulness to the city and the community which it still serves today had only begun.

Though death and disease reduced its staff to the editor and a single printer, The Appeal never missed an issue in this ghastly epidemic.

CHAPTER VIII

Yellow Fever Days

IT IS the fateful Summer of 1878 and Memphis is in her hour of bitterest trial.

The dread yellow fever epidemic has come on the sultry wings of August and men, women and children are dying like flies. A hundred yesterday, a hundred more today, and a hundred more, now alive, doomed to die tomorrow. A sudden chill, a blazing fever, retching vomiting, wild delirium, a few hours of merciful unconsciousness, and then the end.

Coffins are stacked high on the street corners, and all night long the dead wagons rumble out the dusty road to Elmwood Cemetery where the grave diggers work overtime. Thousands of the city's population have fled in terror, crowding the trains and every available conveyance in their frantic haste. A noble band of heroes remains behind to nurse the sick and comfort the dying. The streets are practically deserted, except for doctors, nurses and undertakers.

Memphis is a city of the dead.

A bearded, haggard editor sits alone in The Appeal's office. Through the open window the hot breath of August brings the sound he had heard for days ... the creaking of an undertaker's wagon making its rounds as the driver rings a bell and drones monotonously: "Bring out your dead, bring out your dead!" The weary man turns to his desk, picks up his pen and writes an item for the morrow's paper:

"Owing to the fact that Mrs. Brooks, wife of W. S. Brooks,

of the editorial staff of The Appeal, has been taken down with the fever, J. M. Keating is alone on duty. He will be glad of any assistance the citizens can render by sending him local information for these columns.

"All but one of the printers of The Appeal are now absent or down with the fever. The one remaining is Mr. Henry Moode who, besides setting type, has to assist Mr. Richard Smith in superintending the printers' infirmary and is, consequently, absent a good deal during working hours." *

The bearded, haggard man who penned these lines as he sat beneath the hovering shadow of death, not knowing if he himself would be the next to go, was Col. J. M. Keating, The Appeal's famous editor of yellow fever days. It is to his undying credit that although death and pestilence reduced The Appeal's staff to himself and one printer in those ghastly days, the paper never missed an issue although at times it was reduced to a single sheet.

There is perhaps no greater instance of personal heroism in all the annals of American journalism. Here was an editor, when all but himself and a single printer had been claimed by the plague, who stuck to his post of duty to issue a daily newspaper that was so vitally needed by the town's doctors, nurses, the Howard Association and the City Health Department for disseminating information in their gallant fight against Death.

John McLeod Keating, Scottish born and Dublin educated, seems to have inherited some of the cold fire of determination that enabled his predecessors, McClanahan and Dill, to keep the paper alive during the Civil War. His vivid daily accounts in The Memphis Appeal during Memphis' terrible epidemic of 1878 have been compared with Defoe's "Journal of the Plague Year" in their portrayal of grotesque horrors.

Colonel Keating, worthy successor to Van Pelt and McClanahan and Dill, was one of that long line of great editors of what is now The Commercial Appeal. Following Colonel Dill's death in January, 1866, the paper was edited for a time by the distinguished General Albert Pike of Arkansas, Mexican War hero, father of Scottish Rite Masonry and a distinguished lawyer, author and scholar whose memory is now honored with a heroic statue in Washington, D. C. General Pike's retirement in 1868 brought Colonel Keating and Colonel M. C. Gallaway, former Confederate postmaster at Memphis, to the helm as coeditors, and for 20 eventful years they ran The Appeal.

*List of The Appeal's dead on Page VI, Appendix.

They carried The Appeal through the dark days of the Reconstruction Era, fighting successfully for the enfranchisement of former Confederate soldiers and battling the corruption of carpet-bag rule so valiantly that Colonel Gallaway went to jail for his views, rather than recant. Bravely, unselfishly, they labored through the columns of The Appeal to rebuild their city and their community from the ruin the war had wrought.

A decade had passed, they were well along with their task—and then, suddenly, Yellow Jack swept its sickle of death through Memphis' magnolia-lined streets. Between midAugust, when the first feverish victim fell ill, and October, when the frost came and mysteriously ended the scourge as suddenly as it had begun, more than 5000 Memphians died and thousands more were stricken. But there is no mystery about the cessation now, for since that time science has convicted the mosquito as the culprit and yellow fever has been banished from the earth.

As early as July 27, 1878, the Mayor of Memphis had declared a quarantine against New Orleans, Natchez and other cities where yellow fever had developed farther South. The gravity of the situation was well known as Memphis had had lesser epidemics of the fever in 1855 and again in 1873.

But the plague crept up the river and, despite the best efforts of the City Health Department, it crawled into Memphis. On Aug. 13, Mrs. Kate Biondi, whose husband operated a small restaurant on North Front Street that was patronized by rivermen, was taken suddenly ill and died next day. The Health Department publicly diagnosed the case as yellow fever and immediately disinfected the rooms, premises and nearby streets with carbolic acid.

On Aug. 14, 22 new cases were discovered in the city and wild panic followed the announcement. Every train leaving Memphis departed with all seats taken and passengers crowded into the aisles and hanging to the platforms; others fled in wagons, buggies and even on horseback. Within three days, 20,000 white people had hurriedly left the city and the Board of Health advised the others to depart as the only hope of checking the spread of the epidemic was by depopulation. Many, however, remained, and among them were the employes of The Appeal.

Yellow Jack came on, sweeping his sickle of death in ever widening circles. On the morning of Aug. 24, The Appeal reported 306 cases of fever in the city, 96 deaths, and the epidemic gaining fast. Two of the saddest cases were those of Mrs. John

Donovan and Mrs. Beno Hollenberg. The former, 12 hours after being taken ill, was delivered of a still-born babe, and the latter gave birth to a fine, healthy child.

Soon Memphis was quarantined by every other city for miles around. The nearest that the railroad trains from the West would come, for example, was Forrest City, Ark. Persons who tried to flee to other cities were turned back by shotgun squads.

By Aug. 26, the number of cases had grown to 573 and the deaths to 140, despite the fact that the Health Department was frantically drenching the streets in the infected area with barrels of carbolic acid. At night the sky was aglow from the fires of bedding and other effects of the victims as these effects were being burned in the streets. Inch by inch, column by column, grew The Appeal's list of the daily dead.

There were many terrible cases. A man walking down Poplar Street was nearly sickened by the nauseating stench coming from a building near the bayou. Bursting in the door, he found the dead body of the occupant lying on a bed. A dead mother was found, her babe crying at her cold breast. Investigation of a sickening odor in the rear of The Appeal's office led to the discovery, in an outhouse, of the body of a negro woman who had been dead several days and whose corpse was half eaten by rats. There were many such cases.

In the common horror, the lines of caste and creed disappeared. White man and black man labored heroically, side by side. Women who were rich and women who were poor volunteered as nurses as they extended the hand of mercy to cool fevered brows. Protestant minister and Catholic priest toiled without stint as they comforted the sick and brought the blessed assurance of Jesus to the dying. Annie Cook, painted madame of the city's most palatial demimonde establishment, ousted her girl inmates overnight and converted her place into a hospital, remaining there to nurse the sick until she fell ill and died.

No tolling church bells broke the deathly silence of the stricken city, for all congregations had been dispersed. Business houses were closed, their owners having fled. Dead wagons rumbled slowly through the empty streets, undertakers ringing their bells and droning "Bring out your dead, bring out your dead!"

Amid such scenes of grisly horror, the heroic Colonel Keating, putting out The Appeal with the aid of a single printer, worked 16 hours a day as he alternated between editorial desk and type case. He wrote in the shadow of death, not knowing if he would be the next to go, and here are some of the items that trailed from his vivid pen—

Aug. 28—"Ninety-six new cases and 32 deaths is the Board of Health's appalling report today . . . The close, damp, disagreeable weather is increasing its ravages and the scarcity of nurses and physicians is leaving cases entirely at the mercy of this disease. It is blood-curdling to listen to the details of the heart-rending incidents they encounter in various parts of the city . . . Whole families have been swept out of existence—father, mother and children have followed each other in rapid succession to the grave."

Sept. 1—"We believe the new cases of yesterday will reach 200. The region of the city known as the infected district is now so nearly depopulated by death and desertion that few new cases are being reported from that quarter. The great increase in numbers now is from the Ninth Ward (northern part of the city, called Chelsea) which shows that the contagion has taken a firmer grasp in that locality."

Sept. 3—"There is now no part of the corporate limits of the city not thoroughly infected with the fever poison. All Sunday and yesterday hearses followed each other at a trot to the cemetery, unattended by any but the hearse drivers. Even this was not fast enough and corpses accumulated in various parts of the city until the fearful stench became alarmingly offensive."

Sept. 7—"To lose over 1200 men, women and children in 27 days out of a population of 19,000 white and black who remain, and to be expending over $10,000 for 1200 nurses and 40 doctors, and for medicines and food for more than 3000 sick and 10,000 indigent is a sad reality—enough to move even the most stoic to tears . . . But besides this there have come tales of individual sorrow, of whole families being swept away in a week, leaving not even one of the name; of nurses dying at their posts, of priests and good Sisters following those they succored so fast as to appall the stoutest heart and give us pause amid the general wreck and ruin. No pen can do these sights and scenes justice; no tongue can exaggerate them. Lisping childhood, hoary and venerable old age, the vagrant, the man of God and the unbeliever—all are taken and claimed alike by this awful pestilence."

Sept. 7—"In this office, as we write, there are but two left of all who were a month ago employed in the editorial, counting and composing rooms, and our pressman is down with the fever.

Col. J. M. Keating (left), then editor of The Appeal, was the great journalistic hero of Memphis' terrible yellow fever epidemic of 1878 which claimed more than 5000 lives. Though death and disease reduced the paper's staff to the editor and one printer, it never missed an issue during the plague.

—Illustration Courtesy Cossitt Library Reference Department

Strangers to the office, as to our business, are attending to our affairs, while the only editor left on duty alternates, through 16 hours a day, between desk and type case. Our experience is one that we shall never forget, and yet it is a common one."

Sept. 8—"Worse and worse has the epidemic grown. Fear sits on every face and dread lies in every heart. Hope, we have none. We despair of any relief, but are nerved for the end. We pray blessings upon the generous who have helped us in all the states; we pray for the safety of those who have come among us to nurse the sick and minister to the dying, and we ask that the names of the women and men who have laid down their lives for us shall be handed down forever as among the best and brightest on earth."

Sept. 9—"This epidemic surpasses all others in the horrors uncovered. Men have dropped dead on the streets, while others have died neglected, only to be discovered by the death-spreading gases from their bodies. Little children crying for food she could no longer give have appealed to their dead mother. Ministers of the gospel, hurrying from house to house, have had their feet stayed and their work arrested by the pestilence that stalks in the noon-day as well as at night. The priest, administering the extreme unction, and the bride of Christ, wiping the death-damp from the forehead of those whose friends and kinfolk are far away, are almost paralyzed in the sacred act and die even before they know they are sick."

Sept. 9—"Parents have deserted children, husbands their wives, but not one wife a husband."

Sept. 10—"Dr. Mitchell, the city health officer, reports 636 new cases of yellow fever have been reported for the 48 hours embracing Sunday and Monday."

Sept. 11—"Among the heroes, there are cowards. Yesterday, a man deserted his sick wife and their children; if this scoundrel isn't dead yet, someone ought to shoot him."

Sept. 12—"Rev. E. C. Slater has gone to his reward as a faithful servant of Christ. He died yesterday. No man did more than he on behalf of the sick. He was a true Christian. No one knew him but to love him, and none can name him but to praise."

Sept. 12—"Let it be recorded to their credit that the negro militia and policemen have discharged their duties zealously and with discretion. We are proud of them. They have proved their title to the gratitude of the people of Memphis."

Sept. 20—"The following is a copy of a telegram sent to New York, to be read at Booth's Theater on the 21st inst.: 'Deaths to date, 2250; number sick now, about 3000; average deaths, 60 per cent of the sick. We are feeding 10,000 persons, sick and destitute, in camps in the city. Fifteen volunteer physicians have died, 20 others are ill. A great many nurses have died. We are praying for frost; it is our only hope. A thousand thanks to the good people of New York for their kind aid."

And so ran the news in the darkest hour in Memphis' long story, penned by the editor of The Appeal and captured for history by the thin old files.

There were heroes aplenty, and none performed braver service than Memphis' Catholic priests and Catholic sisters, many of whom paid with their lives. Into the homes of rich and poor they went, regardless of danger, extending the gentle hand of mercy to the suffering and bringing comforting solace to the dying. Among these heroic martyrs of the clergy was the beloved Father Riordan, pastor of St. Patrick's Church, and of his death The Appeal said on Sept. 18:

"The Very Rev. M. Riordan, vicar-general of this diocese and pastor of St. Patrick's Church, died yesterday morning after two weeks' illness from the fever. Like those of his brethren in the priesthood who preceded him, he fell at his post. He contracted the disease while in the discharge of the duties of his sacred office and fell as a brave soldier of the cross loves to fall . . . Spent in The Master's service, he leaves his parish in mourning and his brethren in tears."

In all the parade of ghastly horror, there is no more pathetic story than that of Annie Cook, the prostitute. The files of the old Appeal tell how she turned her palatial Gayoso Street "Mansion House" into a hospital and died in the service of mercy. Here is the story they relate:

Sept. 5—"Annie Cook, the keeper of a bagnio on Gayoso Street, who has most heroically devoted herself to the care of the sick since the fever set in, is down with a bad case of the fever. We hope she may recover. No one has done better service than she during the epidemic."

Sept. 12—"Annie Cook, the woman who after a long life of shame ventured all she had of life and property for the sick, died yesterday at 7 o'clock of the fever, which she contracted while nursing her patients.

"If there was virtue in the faith of the woman who but touched the hem of the garment of the Divine Redeemer, surely the sins of this woman must have been forgiven her. Her faith hath made her whole—made her one with the loving Christ whose example she followed in giving her life so that others might live.

"Amid so much that is sorrowful to an agonizing degree, so much that has illumined the graces of a common humanity, and so much that disgraces humanity, the example of this brave woman stands by itself as singular but beautiful, sad, but touching, the very expression of that hope the realization of which we have in the words: 'Inasmuch as ye have done it unto the least of these, my brethren, ye have done it unto me.'

"Out of sin, this woman in all the tenderness and true fullness of her womanhood emerged, transfigured and purified, to become the healer, and at last to come to the Healer of souls, with Him to rest forever. She is at peace."

Came October's frost that killed the mosquitos and Yellow Jack's grisly hand was stayed. But his toll had been a heavy one. Of Memphis' 45,000 population, 25,000 had fled the city and of the 20,000 who remained 17,600 contracted the disease. Of the 6000 white persons who remained in the city, 4204 died and of the 14,000 negroes who remained, among whom the death rate was much lower, 946 perished.

The Appeal had suffered heavily. A final checkup showed that of the paper's employes, 19 were dead, 21 were convalescent, 15 had suffered deaths in their families and 18 had suffered illness in their families—a total of 73. The only two employes of The Appeal who escaped death, illness or sickness in their families were Colonel Keating, the editor, and Henry Moode, printer.

During the epidemic, Colonel Keating's co-editor, Colonel Gallaway, had done yeoman work in touring the North and East, conducting mass meetings and raising money for the relief of the sufferers. Colonel Gallaway raised thousands of dollars in this manner, painting the epidemic's horrors in many cities and exhibiting copies of The Appeal that contained long lists of the daily dead. The response was invariably generous.

But, as with all things, the epidemic had come to an end and The Memphis Appeal turned its face to the future as it began the task of rebuilding the devastated city. The keynote was this striking editorial published on the morning of Oct. 29, addressed to the citizens of Memphis:

"The epidemic is over. The Board of Health officially declares it so, and invites absentees to return. Business doubtless will be fully resumed by the end of the week and by November we will, we have reason to hope, be on the full tide to prosperity again.

"But little cotton has been picked, and of that little comparatively few bales have found their way to market. The trade of Memphis is untouched; the same causes that operated to prevent business in the city have likewise been felt by planters and country merchants. Our business men have only to press their claims in the region of the country where they have hitherto been supreme. . .

"Coming back to their homes and their offices, it is naturally to be expected that some time will be devoted by our citizens to a contemplation of the havoc of the pestilence. Friends will be missed and mourned for, and there will be sorrow and not rejoicing everywhere. But the claims of life are so many and so pressing that little time can be spared for the luxury of indulging in woe. The living claim the need of our instant attention. Happy for us that it is so. Were it otherwise, grief would be a calamity only surpassed by the plague in which it had its origin.

"The treadmill of life will not stop, no matter who falls. The ranks that are thinned today are strengthened tomorrow. The calamities of one hour are forgotten the next. The sea that surges today will break upon the shore tomorrow in ripples so light as scarcely to make a mark.

"We do not forget because we cannot forget, but the forces which are ever working and by which we are ever impelled onward, take us beyond the history of each hour's memories, fading faster and faster, until there is nothing but the shadow resting on the most suffering heart.

"Thus it is that the compensations of life are beneficently ordered. Behind every dark cloud we find the silver lining."

Another epic of heroism, as great as that in the Civil War, had been written in the saga of a newspaper that has now served its community for a hundred years.

On the sure foundation laid by his famous predecessors, a great editor builded what is today "The South's Greatest Newspaper."

CHAPTER IX

The Mooney Era

THE STORY of The Commercial Appeal's one hundred years has been the story of the MidSouth's progress through a century, for the growth and development of what is today "The South's Greatest Newspaper" has been symmetrical with that of the community which it serves.

When Memphis was a sprawling little river hamlet back in 1840, Col. Henry Van Pelt, The Appeal's first editor, scribbled with his quill pen by the light of a tallow candle in his tiny frame building on the muddy banks of Wolf River. When the Civil War flamed in the 1860's and Memphis was captured by the Yankees, The Appeal and its readers suffered alike. When the ghastly yellow fever epidemic swept Memphis in 1878, The Appeal's list of dead was proportionate to that of the city.

Hand in hand, through peace and war and panic and plenty, this newspaper and its five generations of readers have traveled down the long avenue of the years together.

In 1840, when young Memphians were shooting squirrels on the present site of Hotel Gayoso, The Appeal was founded. In 1866, when Memphis was thrilled by its first mule cars, The Appeal moved into a new and larger building. In 1872, when the city government took steps to curb hogs and cows that were roaming at large in the streets, The Appeal got a new double-cylinder press to replace the old single-cylinder Hoe that had fought the Civil War on many fronts.

In the early 1890's, about the time the first electric arc lights were beginning to sputter on Main Street, The Appeal became the first newspaper in the South to install linotype machines. In December, 1899, when the Spanish-American War was but a recent memory, it bought a big new press and on April 15, 1900, it became the first newspaper in the South to print a Sunday comic section—remember "Happy Hooligan," "Foxy Grandpa" and "The Katzenjammer Kids"? In 1923 it went on the air with its own radio station, WMC, and in 1926—just 78 years after it had introduced telegraphic news service to Memphis in 1848—came the first telephoto and the receipt of news pictures by wire, a picture of General Lee's gigantic statue carved on Stone Mountain in Georgia. On Jan. 1, 1940, in commemorating its 100th anniversary, it issued a 328-page Centennial Edition, the largest week-day newspaper ever published in the United States and containing more than 1000 columns of news material.

To attempt to detail all the other improvements that have marked The Commercial Appeal's steady progress through a hundred years would be a limitless task. Still, in looking back over the parade of a century, one cannot forget how The Commercial Appeal and the New York Herald "scooped" the world on Admiral Dewey's smashing victory over the Spanish Fleet in the Battle of Manila Bay in 1898; how, in 1906, The Commercial Appeal, in co-operation with the New York Times and the London Times, printed Commander Peary's exclusive story of his discovery of the North Pole and the conquest of a dream of three centuries; how, in 1911, The Commercial Appeal paid a $5000 cash prize to Roland Garros, daring Frenchman, for being the first man to fly an airplane over Memphis, and that this same Garros was both the hero and the victim of the first air battle in the world's history when he drove his plane broadside into a German Zeppelin early in August, 1914, both crashing in flames . . . That story is endless.

Like the stricken city itself, The Memphis Appeal began to rebuild after the terrible yellow fever epidemic of 1878 and its progress was similarly rapid. With long strides grew the population and the wealth of one, the circulation and prestige of the other. Still at the helm were the co-editors, Colonel Keating and Colonel Gallaway, who ran the paper for 20 years.

In 1887, Colonel Gallaway, then 70, decided to retire and The Appeal was sold to a local syndicate headed by Capt. W. A. Collier, a grand old hero of the Confederacy who had ridden with

Forrest's cavalry. The following year, Colonel Keating resigned from The Appeal and Captain Collier took full charge.

There were two morning newspapers in Memphis then, The Appeal and The Avalanche, and The Avalanche was on the wane. In 1889 a third morning paper entered the field, The Memphis Commercial, with Col. W. J. Crawford as its publisher and Colonel Keating as its editor. Bright, vigorous and aggressive, The Commercial made rapid gains.

In November, 1890, The Appeal took over The Avalanche under the name of The Appeal-Avalanche and introduced a number of improvements, including a Sunday magazine section which contained stories by a young author who showed great promise. His name was Robert Louis Stevenson. Two years later the aging Colonel Keating retired from the editorship of The Commercial and Edward Ward Carmack, one of the most brilliant writers the South has ever produced, came over from Nashville to take charge.

In 1894 The Commercial bought The Appeal-Avalanche and on the morning of July 1 that year the first issue of The Commercial Appeal appeared. Thus this newspaper took its present name and began sowing the seeds of the great morning journal of the MidSouth that it is today.

In 1896 a rising young politician named William Jennings Bryan electrified the Democratic Convention at Chicago with his famous "Cross of gold and crown of thorns" speech, and Editor Carmack followed "the boy orator of the Platte" into the paths of free silver. But the owners of the paper were in favor of the gold policy, differences immediately came to a head and overnight Carmack resigned. He left his editorial chair to begin his remarkable career in American politics which was marked by his election to the United States Senate and climaxed by his assassination on a Nashville street, as the result of a political quarrel, in 1908.

With the departure of Carmack, a bright young man from the old Evening Scimitar came to The Commercial Appeal as its managing editor—and thus began "The Mooney Era" that illumined The Commercial Appeal's story for 20 years.

Charles Patrick Joseph Mooney was a Kentuckian who had passed a year or so on a small daily paper at Pine Bluff, Ark., before coming to Memphis. He was equally eloquent with pen or tongue, and gifted with a vision a full generation ahead of his time that was backed by driving energy and limitless ability. Immediately, he set out to make The Commercial Appeal the greatest newspaper in the South.

His first big opportunity came in the Spanish-American War when, at an expense that then seemed fabulous, he hooked up with The New York Herald in the sending of a special correspondent to the Philippines and "scooped the world" on the Battle of Manila Bay. When the State Supreme Court issued its historic 75,000-word decision on the Cooper-Carmack case in 1909, he leased every one of the 18 circuits that the Western Union and the Postal Telegraph Co. operated between Memphis and Nashville and got every word of the voluminous decision in the next morning's paper. In similar ways he added rapidly to the prestige of The Commercial Appeal.

Mooney's theory of how to put out a newspaper was illustrated on the occasion of Commander Peary's discovery of the North Pole. The New York Times had exclusive rights to the famous explorer's own story of his discovery, wirelessed from the Far North, and offered The Commercial Appeal the story at a high price. Bill Adler, telegraph editor, received the telegram containing the offer and took it to his chief.

"Go ahead and order it, Bill," said Mr. Mooney, "it's great stuff."

"But chief," demurred Adler, "look at this price they're asking——"

"Never mind about the cost, Bill," replied Mr. Mooney. "Go ahead and buy it. Nothing is too good for our readers. Put out a good newspaper and expenses will take care of themselves."

Only one interval broke Mr. Mooney's long service. In 1902 he went to New York, but in 1908 he returned and resumed the editorship with renewed vigor.

For the next 18 years, until his death in 1926, the story of The Commercial Appeal was largely the story of C. P. J. Mooney. He came in an era when Memphis was a city of barely over 100,000 population and The Commercial Appeal was struggling to establish itself as a metropolitan daily. He went out in an era when Memphis, with a population of over 200,000, was firmly entrenched as the MidSouth capital that it is today, and The Commercial Appeal was recognized as one of America's leading newspapers.

Mr. Mooney's famous editorial, "Jesus, The Perfect Man," is on Page VII, Appendix

For 20 years the story of The Commercial Appeal was the story of C. P. J. Mooney, one of the most famous editors in the paper's century-old history. He builded "The South's Greatest Newspaper" of today.

Upon that growing community and that changing region, C. P. J. Mooney left his mark as his editorial pen wrote with an ink that, so history has proved, was indelible.

With a vision that was far ahead of his time, and with the courage and ability to match it, he campaigned editorially—in the very heart of the cotton region—for diversified farming which, he insisted, would liberate the South from the fickle mercy of the one-crop system and give it a sounder economic base. Back in 1912 and 1913 the cotton farmers laughed at Mooney's vigorous editorials, but Mooney kept on. By the early 1920's, when cotton prices began to hit the skids, they were saying that maybe Mr. Mooney was right, after all. In 1932, when cotton sank to less than five cents a pound on the Memphis market, they realized he had been right, all along.

Today there is a monument to C. P. J. Mooney on nearly every farm in the MidSouth. It is no ornate carving of silent stone; it is a towering silo, a well-filled feed barn, a herd of fat cattle grazing in the pasture, a neat white dairy barn, or, perhaps, row upon row of home-canned foods in a thrifty farmwife's basement. These are Mr. Mooney's monuments.

Under Mooney's virile editorship, The Commercial Appeal was a tower of strength for every worthy cause. In times of flood and disaster it was first into the field, gathering the news and raising funds for the relief of the sufferers. It campaigned for morality in politics, for better schools for the MidSouth's children, for stronger levees to protect its fertile farms, for measures that would promote public health, for a free bridge across the Mississippi River at Memphis, for every forward-looking movement.

When the World War came along in 1917, Mr. Mooney dedicated the columns of The Commercial Appeal to the patriotic cause of its country. He violated all rules by running advertisements on Page 1—advertisements urging the public to buy Liberty Bonds. His trenchant editorials fanned the MidSouth's patriotism to a white hot flame, interpreted the shift of mighty events in a trembling world with analytical keenness.

Just as others had in the Mexican War, the Civil War and the Spanish-American War, 37 employes of The Commercial Appeal answered the call to the colors in that conflict, prominent among them being the late Capt. Thomas Fauntleroy, later the paper's managing editor. Two of these 37 made the supreme sacrifice—Capt. Gordon Gillespie, a reporter, was killed in action while leading a charge against the German trenches; Frank Giardina, an office boy, died far from home of wounds received while fighting with a British outfit.

An outstanding figure of the Mooney era was the late J. P. Alley, who became one of America's most famous cartoonists. Alley was a Benton, Ark., boy who had a flair for drawing. He came to Memphis, got a job with an engraving company as an artist, and there Mooney found him. His rise to journalistic heights under Mr. Mooney's keen tutelage was as swift as it was sensational.

Before, after and during the World War, J. P. Alley's front-page cartoons in The Commercial Appeal were a daily feature as they mirrored the political and other issues of the day with razor-edged keenness. Enthusiastic Southern congressmen clipped them and posted them over the marble mantel in the Democratic cloakroom at the Nation's Capitol. Arthur Brisbane praised them as "the work of one of America's greatest cartoonists." Others were as unstinted in their praise as Alley's fame continued to spread.

But Jim Alley's virile drawing pen that could (and often did) make or break a major political issue also had another facet. Still remembered for its eye-moistening depth of pathos is his famous Community Fund cartoon of 1927 in which he pictured a humble old negro porter who was reminding his boss to "drap some'pin in de box for de pore folks." A Memphis woman was so impressed by that cartoon that she paid $200 for the original, Alley giving the money to the Community Fund. In the same spirit Jim Alley created and syndicated "Hambone," that philosophical Southern darkey who lives today in the drawings of Alley's sons.

It was a fitting tribute to both Mr. Mooney and Mr. Alley that their joint efforts—Mooney's powerful editorials and Alley's keen-edged cartoons—won for The Commercial Appeal in 1923 the highest honor in American journalism, the Pulitzer prize. It is awarded annually "for the most disinterested and meritorious public service rendered by any American newspaper during the year." It was their smashing campaign against the bigotry and intolerance of the Ku Klux Klan, and its flogging of helpless victims by masked men, that brought this recognition.

On Nov. 22, 1926, Mr. Mooney's editorial labors came to an

end. He expired, of a sudden stroke, while working at his desk. He was writing an editorial at the time.

C. P. J. Mooney died, perhaps, as he would have liked to have died—to the requiem of the chattering typewriters of the reporters, the noisy clatter of the telegraph instruments that were wafting in the world's news, the clicking of the busy linotype machines and the muffled roar of the mighty presses.

So ended another era in the hundred-year-old history of The Commercial Appeal, the era of a man who worked miracles of journalism and made it, in truth as in word, "The South's Greatest Newspaper." But before The Commercial Appeal lay another era, the one which brings us down to now.

More than a newspaper, The Commercial Appeal is today a Southern institution, welcomed in the homes of readers for five generations.

CHAPTER X

Down To Now

WHEN COL. HENRY VAN PELT unfurled his journalistic banner to the breeze and founded the tiny Memphis Weekly Appeal with an old Washington handpress and a few cases of dusty type a hundred years ago, it is doubtful if his fondest dreams could have exceeded what has since become a reality.

The Commercial Appeal today is one of America's greatest newspapers. This statement does not represent self-adulation but, rather, the appraisal of others.

Time Magazine has picked The Commercial Appeal as "one of the 14 great American newspapers." The others so named are the New York Times, the Chicago Daily News, the Atlanta Constitution, the Baltimore Sun, the Chicago Tribune, the Christian Science Monitor, the Dallas News, the Detroit News, the Kansas City Star, the Los Angeles Times, the New York Daily News, the New York Herald-Tribune and the St. Louis Post-Dispatch.

The library of the University of Chicago has chosen The Commercial Appeal as one of the 12 American newspapers for future historical and social science reference—the newspapers, chemically preserved, that researchers seeking light on our times will consult centuries hence. The 11 other newspapers so chosen are: the Portland Oregonian, the Los Angeles Times, the Minneapolis Journal, the Omaha World-Herald, the Detroit News, the New Orleans Times-Picayune, the Atlanta Constitution, the Richmond News-Ledger, the Cleveland Plain Dealer, the Denver News and the Toronto Globe.

Acclaimed today, preserved for generations yet unborn is the double honor won by The Commercial Appeal.

The story of that success is the story of men, for it is men who are in tune with their times who make great newspapers. In the wake of Van Pelt, who struggled to establish his four-page weekly in a pioneer river hamlet, came McClanahan and Dill who figuratively beat their one-cylinder press into swords and fought the Civil War as bravely as any Confederate soldier; in their wake came Keating, the great journalistic hero of yellow fever days; in his wake came the eloquent Carmack, alive to the problems of a South that was swiftly changing from plantation feudalism to modernity; and in his wake came Mooney who, with a vision a full generation ahead of his time, foresaw and helped build the South of today. In the wake of these have come the men who labor to get out the paper of the present, and in their wake will come other men who are as yet still unborn.

For the hundred-year-old history of The Commercial Appeal has demonstrated that it is more than a newspaper, it is a Southern institution. Times change, men appear upon the stage to play their parts like actors and then retire, but the paper goes on. New actors appear, the scenery shifts in accord with the changing era, but the play is never ended.

In May, 1927, a short time after Mr. Mooney's death, The Commercial Appeal was bought by Luke Lea and Rogers Caldwell of Nashville, who were then building a chain of Southern newspapers. After various managements and certain financial reverses, the paper was finally restored to a stable ownership on June 12, 1933, through its purchase by Col. James Hammond, a former banker of Lake Village, Ark., who had won success in New York financial circles.

Under Colonel Hammond's direction the paper quickly resumed its progress. New departments were added, new services and equipment purchased and new enterprises undertaken. Outstanding among the latter was The Commercial Appeal's Plant to Prosper Competition which implemented the doctrine of farm diversification and home-grown food and feed crops that Mooney had preached for 20 years. Begun with 1800 contestants in 1934,

Plant to Prosper's success has been so sweeping that, through The Commercial Appeal and other Southern newspapers to which it has been extended, it now enrolls upwards of 50,000 Dixie farmers in its live-at-home aims, and is still growing.

But Plant to Prosper has meant something much greater than merely increased food and feed crops in the South's cotton belt; for many farmers who had struggled along with a single crop for years it has spelled economic independence, better homes, more comforts for their families, and more opportunities and better education for their children.

Perhaps those who conceived Plant to Prosper and coined its catchy name in 1934 had in mind a man like H. L. Majure of Poplar Grove, Ark., the 1938 sweepstakes winner. For 18 years Mr. Majure had been a sharecropper, living in drafty cabins, burdened by debt to his landlord and eking out a meager existence for his family. Today, after applying the principles of Plant to Prosper, Mr. Majure has a 40-acre farm of his own, a modern six-room bungalow with electric lights and a refrigerator purring in the kitchen, a pasture full of fat livestock and a barn full of feed. And the last note on the mortgage was paid more than a year ago.

The success of its Plant to Prosper movement has brought to The Commercial Appeal national and even world-wide recognition, as many see in it the solution to the Cotton South's multiplying economic problems. Articles descriptive of Plant to Prosper's work have been published in several national magazines and letters have been received from agronomists in Spain, Australia, England and Hungary who are considering its application among their own one-crop farmers.

In the Fall of 1936 two great American journalistic institutions were united when The Commercial Appeal was purchased by the Scripps-Howard Newspapers, founded a half century ago upon the liberal policies of the late E. W. Scripps and now carried on by Roy W. Howard, senior trustee. Thus two of the most venerable institutions in the Nation's history of journalism were joined, the ideals and spirit that motivated the one being an integral part of the other.

There was much akin in the stories of their growth from humble beginnings. The Commercial Appeal, founded as a four-page weekly, had developed into the South's greatest newspaper. From the tiny seed that E. W. Scripps had planted as "The

The Commercial Appeal today is published in one of the largest and most modern newspaper plants in the United States. In 1939 more than $350,000 was expended for improvements, including huge new presses.

Penny Press" in Cleveland, Ohio, many years before had grown the long chain of Scripps-Howard Newspapers that stretches from New York to San Francisco.

With this acquisition, John H. Sorrells, formerly of Pine Bluff, Ark., who had risen from the ranks to become executive editor of all the Scripps-Howard newspapers, became president and publisher of The Commercial Appeal. Mr. Sorrells, born in Pine Bluff, got his first newspaper job there as a local carrier boy for The Commercial Appeal. Following experience as a reporter and editor on the Pine Bluff Graphic, a paper founded by his grandfather, he joined Scripps-Howard in Cleveland and was sent to Memphis in 1926 as the first managing editor of the newly merged Press-Scimitar. After a period as editor of the Fort Worth Press, he was made executive editor of all the organization's newspapers.

Capt. Enoch Brown Jr., long identified with the business side of The Commercial Appeal, was retained as vice president and general manager. Frank R. Ahlgren, formerly managing editor of the Evening Appeal (published from 1926 until 1933) and who had been city editor and news editor of The Commercial Appeal, was made executive editor, later editor. The paper of today is published under their direction.

For many years The Commercial Appeal has had the largest circulation of any newspaper in the South, which now runs around 125,000 daily and 150,000 on Sunday. Since 1933 it has occupied its present five-story, steel and concrete building at Union Avenue and the Southern Railway, one of the largest and most modern and best equipped newspaper plants in the United States. In 1939 more than $350,000 was spent for new presses and other improvements. Its new block-long presses, mechanical marvels of thundering speed and hair-line precision, can print up to 256 pages at one operation. The half-million dollars' worth of newsprint that the paper buys each year is unloaded from railroad cars that enter the big building's first floor on a special spur track, while ink is purchased by the tankcarload and pumped to the press reservoirs by means of a threeinch pipe line.

Where Editor Henry Van Pelt used his nimble shears to clip his news from papers brought by friendly steamboat captains a hundred years ago, the three great world-wide press services— the Associated Press, the United Press and the International

News Service—now supply The Commercial Appeal with more than 150,000 words of telegraph news each day, of which only the best is used. Three hundred regional correspondents are on duty in MidSouth cities, towns and villages, while a score of reporters gather the local news. The news edited and headlined by a dozen copy readers. Supplementing these are editorial writers, market writers, sports writers, society writers and a staff of photographers and artists for picturizing the day's most important news events.

Editorial, business, circulation and mechanical departments considered, The Commercial Appeal has on its pay roll in its Memphis plant slightly more than 400 employes. This, of course, does not include the 300 regional correspondents, the circulation agents and their employes in these towns, and the 500 carrier boys who deliver The Commercial Appeal to Memphis homes each morning. It is a fair estimate that, all told, approximately 3000 persons derive direct income from The Commercial Appeal in one form or another.

Twenty-four hours a day, from one end of the world to the other, The Commercial Appeal stands guard over the news. It comes flashing over the telegraph wires or emanates from the clattering typewriters of reporters or correspondents. Editors and copy readers quickly edit the stories and write the headlines; the clicking linotype machines transform "copy" into columns of type; the makeup men place the type in the page forms; the stereotypers roll their "mats" and cast their curved plates from these papier-mache impressions; the metal plates are bolted on the cylinders of the huge presses, a switch is thrown, the deep rumbling roar of meshed steel begins, and the news-wet papers cascade forth. From story to street, in times of necessity, this swift journey can be made in only a few minutes.

The largest week-day newspaper ever published in the United States—and the largest paper in history except for a Sunday issue published by a Miami newspaper during the Florida boom—The Commercial Appeal's 328-page Centennial Edition on Jan. 1, 1940 marked the climax of its first century and its salute to its second. Record breaking in content as well as in volume, the Centennial Edition contained more than 1000 columns of news matter and pictures prepared under the direction of its editor, Robert Talley, and nearly 500,000 lines of advertising, sold under the direction of its advertising manager, A. C. Bailey.

Such is the story of The Commercial Appeal today, and

such is the story of the 100 years of steady progress that lie behind it. From the day in 1840 when Col. Henry Van Pelt first unfurled his journalistic banner to the breeze down to this good hour, this newspaper has been the loyal friend and the faithful servant of five generations of MidSouth readers, sharing with them in times of triumph and in times of adversity.

And so The Commercial Appeal—not merely a newspaper but an institution in the community which it serves—ends its first one hundred years. It is proud of its traditions and its heritage, pardonably proud. Its greatest aim for the future is to be as good a friend and neighbor in the next century as it has been in the one just ended.

APPENDIX

Headlines that made history, taken from the old files . . . there have been many such in 100 years.

"God Bless Memphis!"
Wept Mark Twain

Of all the terrible steamboat disasters that made the Mississippi a river of tears in the old days, none was more tragic than that of the Steamer Pennsylvania, whose boilers exploded a few miles below Memphis, bringing sudden death to scores and horribly scalding many others, including Henry Clemens, youngest brother of the famous Mark Twain (Samuel Clemens).

The Memphis Appeal of June 18, 1858, told the story of this great disaster, and listed the names of the suffering victims who were rushed here for medical attention. In the "List of Injured at the Exchange," the following line appeared: "Henry Clemens of St. Louis, third clerk; badly scalded."

The great Mark Twain, who chanced to be coming up the river as a pilot on another boat at the time, heard the news at Greenville, Miss., and rushed to his dying brother's bedside. Here is the heart-rending letter that he wrote to his family:

Memphis, Tenn., June 21, 1858.

Dear Sister Mollie:
Long before this reaches you, my poor Henry—my darling, my pride, my glory, my all—will have finished his blameless career, and the light of my life will have gone out in utter darkness.

The horrors of three days have swept over me—they have blasted my youth and left me an old man before my time. Mollie, there are gray hairs in my head tonight. For 48 hours I labored at the bedside of my poor, burned, bruised but uncomplaining brother, and then the star of my hope went out and left me in the gloom of despair. Men take me by the hand and congratulate me, and call me "Lucky" because I was not on the Pennsylvania when she blew up! May God forgive them, for they know not what they say.

I was on the Pennsylvania five minutes before she left New Orleans, and I must tell you the truth, Mollie—300 human beings perished in that fearful disaster. But may God bless Memphis, the noblest city on the face of the earth! She has done her duty by these poor, afflicted creatures—especially Henry, for he has had five—aye, ten, fifteen, TWENTY times—the care and attention that anyone else has had.

Dr. Peyton, the best physician in Memphis (he is exactly like the portraits of Webster) sat by him for 36 hours. There were 32 scalded men in that room, and you would know Dr. Peyton better than I could describe him if you could follow him around and hear each man murmur as he passes, "May the God of heaven bless you, Doctor!"

The ladies have done well, too. The second mate, a handsome, noble-

hearted young fellow, will die. Yesterday, a beautiful girl of 15 stooped timidly down by his side and handed him a pretty bouquet. The poor, suffering boy's eyes kindled, his lips quivered out a gentle "God bless you, Miss," and he burst into tears. He made them write her name on a card for him, that he might not forget it.

Pray for me, Mollie, and pray for my poor, sinless brother.

Your unfortunate brother,

SAML. L. CLEMENS.

P. S.—I got here two days after Henry.

But, alas, this was not all, nor the worst. The final draft that would embitter the cup of the great Mark Twain was added on the eighth night after the disaster—the night that Henry died. The great author could never bring himself up to write it. He was never known to speak of it thereafter but twice.

What happened next we now quote from Albert Bigelow Paine's "Biography of Mark Twain:"

"He saw the boy taken to the dead room, then the long strain of grief, the days and nights without sleep, the ghastly realization of the end overcame him. A citizen of Memphis took him away in a kind of daze and gave him a bed in his house, where he fell into a stupor of fatigue and surrender.

"It was many hours before he woke; when he did, at last, he dressed and went to where Henry lay. The coffin provided for the dead was of unpainted wood, but the youth and striking face of Henry Clemens had aroused special interest. The ladies of Memphis made up a fund of $60 and bought him a metallic casket."

"In many ways," says Albert Bigelow Paine's biography, "Mark Twain never overcame the tragedy of Henry's death. He never really looked young again. Gray hairs had come, as he said, and they did not disappear. . . . At 23, he looked 30. At 30, he looked nearer 40. After that, the discrepancy in age and looks became less noticeable."

Here is the historic editorial with which The Memphis Appeal greeted the birth of the Confederate States of America, in its issue of Feb. 12, 1861, under the caption of "The Birth of a New Nation."

The Birth Of A New Nation

SATURDAY, the ninth day of February, eighteen hundred and sixty-one, will long be signalized in the calendar of time as the birth of a new nationality.

Upon it an event has transpired whose full realization the intellect can scarcely grasp—an actuality chronicled which but 10 years since Mr. Webster pronounced "an impossibility that had only been dreamed of in the wildest flights of human imagination." The skepticism of the statesmen, the despotism of tyranny, and the carping of political croakers to the contrary, a new people, a free nation, a sovereign independency, lives and has its being in THE CONFEDERATED STATES OF NORTH AMERICA!

The convention which assembled at Montgomery on the fourth inst. has not been tardy in its work of political parturition. Seven republics, formerly connected with the United States of America, but having dissolved the ties binding them under one government, through their representatives have met in solemn council, and pledged their fortunes, their lives and their sacred honor to each other's defense and protection.

Invested with plenary power to construct a provisional government upon the basis of the old Federal Constitution, they have performed the functions of their offices with commendable alacrity. Everything has been done, even to the election of officials, which may be regarded as at all necessary to consummate its perfection. The wonderful, anomalous and sublime aspect is thus presented of a young and vigorous nation springing to life from the womb of a bloodless and peaceful revolution.

We do not propose to go into the details of an overwrought and speculative picture of the brilliant future with which a "manifest destiny" has promised to crown it. With an area of over five hundred thousand square miles, and a population of over three millions of souls, even without the acquisition of border slave states, it begins a full-grown nation.

The population is as large as that of the whole United States Government at the close of the American Revolution; the area nearly three times that of Great Britain or Prussia, twice as large as France and three times larger than all Germany. Its resources, consisting of cotton, rice, sugar, coal and minerals, constitute elements of wealth which are absolute necessities to the civilized world.

Disenthralment from a financial, commercial and political vassalage to a dominant power which will amply serve for their speedy development has come and a new era has dawned upon the South. Material wealth, religious freedom and political equality are now her heritage otherwise than in the mere emptiness of a name. Her sons may well rejoice in having broken the chains forged for their servitude. United, free and prosperous, they are no longer the deluded victims of disaffection and internecine jars, but

> *"Those opposed eyes,*
> *Which, like the meteors of a troubled heaven,*
> *Of all one nature, of one substance bred,*
> *Did lately meet in intestine shock,*
> *Shall now, in mutual, well-beseeming ranks,*
> *MARCH ALL ONE WAY."*

The Memphis Appeal, "The Greatest Rebel of Them All," so ardently supported the Southern Cause that it recruited and equipped a battery of artillery for the Confederate Army.

The Appeal Battery

IN ALL the hundred-year history of The Commercial Appeal, there is no more colorful story than that of The Appeal Battery which was recruited by this newspaper during the Civil War, and which fought under its colors.

The Appeal Battery was organized in Memphis in the Spring of 1862 by Col. John R. McClanahan, one of the paper's editors, and was presented with a silken flag by the ladies of the city when it departed for Corinth and the front on May 6. It took part in the fierce battle there, and later moved on to Vicksburg, where it helped defend the city in the historic siege, several of its members being killed in action. In the shift of war events, it became a part of an Arkansas outfit.

Captured when Vicksburg fell on July 4, 1863, the members of The Appeal Battery were held prisoner by the Yankees for some time and later paroled at Enterprise, Miss. The battery is honored today by five bronze tablets on the Vicksburg Battlefield, marking the positions from which its muzzle-loading cannon hurled their solid iron balls against the enemy.

One of the tablets reads:

THE APPEAL (ARKANSAS) BATTERY
MAURY'S—FORNEY'S DIV.   ARMY OF VICKSBURG
CAPT. WILLIAM N. HOGG
LIEUT. CHRISTOPHER C. SCOTT
LIEUT. ROBERT N. COTTEN

A detachment of this battery under Lieut. Christopher C. Scott served one three-inch rifle in this position May 18 until about May 30, 1863, when cassion was exploded by fire of the Union batteries and the rifle was moved to a less exposed position. Capt. William N. Hogg was killed on duty in this position, May 19.

In November, 1878, after Memphis' great yellow fever epidemic had ended, The Appeal published this recapitulation of its own dead and convalescent:

THE APPEAL'S DEAD
In Memphis' Terrible Yellow Fever Epidemic of Year 1878

OUR DEAD
George W. Woods, temporary bookkeeper

Composing Room

Maj. W. G. Stephenson	James F. Cummings	Chas. M. Smith
J. B. Barker	B. N. Cutting	George Beamish
B. F. Fuller	L. M. Lorentz	

Press Room

Al Plummer	A. S. Hollenshead	John Kelly Sr.
Frank Plummer	Byron Brooks	John Kelly Jr.
Nick (porter)	Andy Harrington	James Kelly

CONVALESCENTS
Counting Room

Henry White	John S. Fifer	Frank Backus

Editorial Room

Fred Brennan	Eugene W. Moore	W. S. Brooks

Composing Room

H. E. Crandall	T. D. Uzell	H. M. Crowell
John B. Hoskins	H. J. McGrann (foreman)	Ed Schiller
W. W. Stephenson	W. G. Taylor	Frank Beamish

Press Room

Kinch Virgeson	Darius Brooks	H. P. Woodlock (foreman)
Louis Breckenbecker	Sam Ellison	Henry Moore

ESCAPED
J. M. Keating, editor   Henry Moode, compositor

FAMILIES OF OUR EMPLOYES
W. S. Brooks' wife, mother and son dead.
Major Stephenson's two daughters dead, one convalescent.
B. N. Nutting's wife convalescent.
George W. Woods' wife convalescent.
H. M. Crowell's daughter dead, wife and son convalescent.
W. W. Stephenson's wife and two children convalescent.
Ed Schiller's son dead, daughter convalescent.
H. J. McGrann's daughter dead, wife, son and niece convalescent.
H. P. Woodlock's daughter convalescent.
Frank and Al Plummer's father, mother and two sisters dead; a brother and sister convalescent.
Darius Brooks' sister dead, mother convalescent.
Byron Brooks' son dead, wife convalescent.
Kinch Virgeson's wife convalescent.
Andy Harrington's wife dead.

RECAPITULATION

Total employes dead 19
Total employes convalescent 21
Total members of families dead 15
Total members of families convalescent 18

Grand total 73

This famous editorial by C. P. J. Mooney was printed in The Commercial Appeal on Dec. 22, 1912. By request of readers, it has been reprinted many, many times, and here it is again.

Jesus, The Perfect Man

THERE is no other character in history like that of Jesus. As a preacher, as a doer of things, and as a philosopher, no man has ever had the sweep and vision of Jesus.

A human analysis of the human actions of Jesus brings to view a rule of life that is amazing in its perfect detail.

The system of ethics Jesus taught during his earthly sojourn 2000 years ago was true then, has been true in every century since, and will be true forever.

Plato was a great thinker and learned in his age, but his teachings did not stand the test of time. In big things and in little things, time and human experience have shown that he erred.

Marcus Aurelius touched the reflective mind of the world, but he was as cold and as austere as brown marble.

The doctrine of Confucius gave a great nation moral and mental dry rot.

The teachings of Buddha resulted in mental and moral chaos that makes India derelict.

* * *

Mohammed offered a system of ethics which was adopted by millions of people. Now their children live in deserts where once there were cities, along dry rivers where once there was moisture, and in shadows of gray, barren hills where once there was greenness.

Thomas Aquinas was a profound philosopher, but parts of his system have been abandoned.

Francis of Assisi was Christlike in his saintliness, but in some respects he was childish.

Thomas a' Kempis' Imitation of Christ is a thing of rare

beauty and sympathy, but it is, as its name indicates, only an imitation.

Sir Thomas Moore's Utopia is yet a dream and cannot be realized.

Lord Bacon writing on chemistry and medicine under the glasses of the man in a twentieth century laboratory is puerile.

The world's most learned doctors until a hundred and fifty years ago gave dragon's blood and ground dried tails of lizards and shells of eggs for certain ailments. The great surgeons of a hundred years ago bled a man if he were wounded.

Napoleon had the world at his feet for four years, and when he died the world was going on its way as if he had never lived.

Jesus thought little as to property, because he knew there were more important things than property. He measured property and life, the body and soul, at their exact relative value. He taught much as to character, because character was more important than dollars.

Other men taught us to develop systems of government. Jesus taught us so as to perfect the minds of men; Jesus looked at the soul, while other men dwell on more material things.

After the experience of 2000 years, no man can find a flaw in the governmental system outlined by Jesus.

Czar and kaiser, president and socialist, give to its complete merit their admiration.

No man today, no matter whether he follows the doctrine of Mills, Marx or George as to property, can find a false principle in Jesus' theory of property.

* * *

In the duty of man to his fellows, no sociologist has ever approximated the perfection of the doctrine laid down by Jesus in His Sermon on the Mount.

Not all the investigations of chemists, not all the discoveries of explorers, not all the experiences of rulers, not all the historical facts that go to make up the sum of human knowledge on this day in 1912 are in contradiction to one word uttered, or one principle laid down by Jesus.

The human experience of 2000 years shows that Jesus never made a mistake. Jesus never uttered a doctrine that was true at the time and then became obsolete.

Jesus spoke the truth; He lived the truth; and truth is eternal.

History has no record of any other man leading a perfect life or doing everything in logical order. Jesus is the only person whose every action and every utterance strike a true note in the heart of every man born of woman. He never said a foolish thing, never did a foolish act, and never dissembled.

No poet, no dreamer, no philosopher loved humanity with the love that Jesus bore toward all men.

Who, then, was Jesus?

He could not have been merely a man, for there was never a man who had two consecutive thoughts absolutely in truthful perfection.

Jesus must have been what Christendom proclaims Him to be—a divine being—or He could not have been what He was. No mind but an infinite mind could have left behind those things which Jesus gave to the world as a heritage.

19-1878